Diabetic

Air Fryer Cookbook for Beginners

Easy and Flavorful, Delicious Diabetic-Friendly Air Fryer Recipes for Healthy Living

By

Sophie Hayes

Copyright 2023 by Sophie Hayes

All rights reserved.

Copyright Notice: This section asserts that the book is copyrighted in 2023 by **Sophie Hayes**, and all rights are reserved. This means that the author retains exclusive rights to the material and prohibits others from using it without permission.

Disclaimer: This disclaimer emphasizes that the information in the book is protected by copyright law, and unauthorized reproduction or distribution is strictly prohibited. It also states that the author and publisher are not liable for any damages or losses resulting from the material in the book.

Legal Disclaimer: This section reiterates the copyright protection and specifies that the book is intended for personal use only. It explicitly prohibits modifying, distributing, selling, quoting, or paraphrasing any part of the book without permission from the author or publisher.

Notice of Disclaimer: This part underscores that the material in the book is provided for educational and entertainment purposes only. It mentions that the information may have been compiled from various sources and does not guarantee accuracy or reliability. It advises readers to seek professional guidance before attempting any practices described in the book. Finally, it acknowledges that the author is not providing legal, financial, medical, or professional advice and disclaims liability for any direct or indirect damages resulting from the use of the information in the document.

In essence, this notice and disclaimer aim to protect the author's intellectual property rights, clarify the limitations of the content, and make readers aware of the lack of guarantees and professional advice within the book. It serves as a legal statement intended to mitigate potential legal issues related to the book's use and the author's liability.

Table of contents

INTRODUCTION 4

CHAPTER 1: GETTING STARTED WITH AIR FRYING 5

    SECTION 1.1: AN OVERVIEW OF AIR FRYERS 5
    WHAT IS AN AIR FRYER? 5
    HOW DOES AIR FRYING WORK? 5
    SECTION 1.2: TIPS FOR CHOOSING THE RIGHT AIR FRYER 5
    SECTION 1.3: BASIC OPERATING INSTRUCTIONS AND SAFETY PRECAUTIONS 6

CHAPTER 2: DIABETES AND NUTRITION 7

    SECTION 2.1: HOW FOOD AFFECTS BLOOD SUGAR LEVELS 7
    SECTION 2.2: GUIDANCE ON CARBOHYDRATE COUNTING AND PORTION CONTROL 7
    SECTION 2.3: THE IMPORTANCE OF FIBER AND LOW GLYCEMIC INDEX FOODS IN A DIABETIC DIET 7

CHAPTER 3: DIABETIC-FRIENDLY INGREDIENTS 8

    SECTION 3.1: ESSENTIAL DIABETIC-FRIENDLY INGREDIENTS 8
    SECTION 3.2: SUGAR SUBSTITUTES AND HOW TO USE THEM 10
    SECTION 3.3: TIPS FOR REDUCING SALT AND SATURATED FAT IN RECIPES 10

CHAPTER 4: BREAKFAST RECIPES 11

    RECIPE 1: AIR FRIED OATMEAL PANCAKES 11
    RECIPE 2: VEGGIE AND CHEESE OMELETTE 11
    RECIPE 3: GREEK YOGURT PARFAIT WITH BERRIES 12
    RECIPE 4: SPINACH AND MUSHROOM BREAKFAST QUESADILLAS 13
    RECIPE 5: CINNAMON APPLE RINGS 13
    RECIPE 6: AIR FRIED BREAKFAST BURRITOS 14
    RECIPE 7: AIR FRIED BANANA-NUT MUFFINS 15
    RECIPE 8: AIR FRIED VEGGIE HASH BROWNS 15
    RECIPE 9: AIR FRIED BREAKFAST STUFFED PEPPERS 16
    RECIPE 10: AIR FRIED BREAKFAST SAUSAGE AND VEGETABLE SKILLET 17
    RECIPE 11: AIR FRIED BANANA AND BLUEBERRY MUFFINS 17
    RECIPE 12: AIR FRIED BREAKFAST SWEET POTATO HASH 18
    RECIPE 13: AIR FRIED CINNAMON FRENCH TOAST STICKS 19
    RECIPE 14: AIR FRIED BREAKFAST BURRITO BOWL 19
    RECIPE 15: AIR FRIED MINI FRITTATAS 20
    RECIPE 16: AIR FRIED AVOCADO AND EGG BREAKFAST 21
    RECIPE 17: AIR FRIED CINNAMON RAISIN BAGEL CHIPS 21
    RECIPE 18: AIR FRIED SPINACH AND FETA STUFFED MUSHROOMS 22
    RECIPE 19: AIR FRIED BREAKFAST QUINOA BOWL 22
    RECIPE 20: AIR FRIED BREAKFAST QUICHE CUPS 23
    RECIPE 21: AIR FRIED PEANUT BUTTER BANANA TOAST 24

CHAPTER 5: APPETIZERS AND SNACKS 25

    RECIPE 1: CRISPY CHICKPEA SNACK 25
    RECIPE 2: ZUCCHINI FRIES WITH YOGURT DIP 25

- Recipe 3: Guacamole-Stuffed Cherry Tomatoes 26
- Recipe 4: Air Fried Mozzarella Sticks 27
- Recipe 5: Air Fried Stuffed Jalapeño Poppers 27
- Recipe 6: Air Fried Sweet Potato Fries with Chipotle Dip 28
- Recipe 7: Air Fried Buffalo Cauliflower Bites 29
- Recipe 8: Air Fried Stuffed Mushrooms 29
- Recipe 9: Air Fried Cumin-Spiced Carrot Chips 30
- Recipe 10: Air Fried Spicy Cauliflower Bites 31
- Recipe 11: Air Fried Crispy Kale Chips 31
- Recipe 12: Air Fried Garlic Parmesan Wings 32
- Recipe 13: Air Fried Stuffed Bell Peppers 33
- Recipe 14: Air Fried Cinnamon Apple Chips 33
- Recipe 15: Air Fried Stuffed Jalapeño Mushrooms 34
- Recipe 16: Air Fried Avocado Fries 35
- Recipe 17: Air Fried Cajun Spiced Pecans 35
- Recipe 18: Air Fried Mini Caprese Skewers 36
- Recipe 19: Air Fried Edamame with Sea Salt 36
- Recipe 20: Air Fried Buffalo Cauliflower Bites 37
- Recipe 21: Air Fried Coconut Shrimp 38

CHAPTER 6: MAIN COURSES 39

- Recipe 1: Lemon Herb Chicken Thighs 39
- Recipe 2: Balsamic Glazed Salmon 39
- Recipe 3: Turkey and Vegetable Stuffed Bell Peppers 40
- Recipe 4: Air Fried Shrimp Scampi 41
- Recipe 5: Air Fried Teriyaki Tofu Stir Fry 41
- Recipe 6: Air Fried Beef and Broccoli 42
- Recipe 7: Air Fried BBQ Pulled Pork Sandwiches 43
- Recipe 8: Air Fried Vegetable Stir-Fry 43
- Recipe 9: Air Fried Vegetarian Quesadillas 44
- Recipe 10: Air Fried Spicy Tofu and Vegetable Skewers 45
- Recipe 11: Air Fried Stuffed Portobello Mushrooms 45
- Recipe 12: Air Fried Cajun Shrimp and Sausage Skillet 46
- Recipe 13: Air Fried Stuffed Chicken Breasts 47
- Recipe 14: Air Fried Eggplant Parmesan 47
- Recipe 15: Air Fried Pork Tenderloin with Apple Compote 48
- Recipe 16: Air Fried Thai Basil Tofu Stir-Fry 49
- Recipe 18: Air Fried Buttermilk Fried Chicken 50
- Recipe 19: Air Fried Quinoa and Black Bean Stuffed Peppers 51
- Recipe 20: Air Fried Teriyaki Chicken and Vegetable Skewers 51

CHAPTER 7: SIDES AND VEGETABLES 53

- Recipe 1: Roasted Brussels Sprouts with Balsamic Reduction 53
- Recipe 2: Garlic Parmesan Air Fried Asparagus 53
- Recipe 3: Spicy Roasted Cauliflower Bites 54
- Recipe 4: Air Fried Sweet Potato Fries 55
- Recipe 5: Air Fried Garlic Parmesan Brussels Sprouts 55
- Recipe 6: Air Fried Zucchini Chips 56

- Recipe 7: Air Fried Garlic Herb Mushrooms 56
- Recipe 8: Air Fried Buttery Corn on the Cob 57
- Recipe 9: Air Fried Herb-Roasted Potatoes 58
- Recipe 10: Air Fried Green Beans with Almonds 58
- Recipe 11: Air Fried Ratatouille 59
- Recipe 12: Air Fried Honey Glazed Carrots 59
- Recipe 13: Air Fried Lemon Garlic Broccoli 60
- Recipe 14: Air Fried Cilantro Lime Corn 60
- Recipe 15: Air Fried Sesame Ginger Green Beans 61

CHAPTER 8: DESSERTS AND TREATS 62

- Recipe 1: Cinnamon Apple Chips 62
- Recipe 2: Chocolate Avocado Pudding 62
- Recipe 3: Mixed Berry Crisp 63
- Recipe 4: Air Fried Banana Fritters 64
- Recipe 5: Air Fried Mini Churros 64
- Recipe 6: Air Fried Strawberry Shortcake 65
- Nutrition Info (per serving, without powdered sugar): 65
- Recipe 7: Air Fried Peach Cobbler 66
- Recipe 8: Air Fried Peanut Butter Banana Bites 66
- Recipe 9: Air Fried S'mores 67
- Recipe 10: Air Fried Blueberry Hand Pies 67
- Recipe 11: Air Fried Mini Apple Pies 68
- Recipe 12: Air Fried Chocolate Chip Cookies 68
- Recipe 13: Air Fried Lemon Bars 69
- Recipe 14: Air Fried Chocolate-Dipped Strawberries 70
- Recipe 15: Air Fried Oreo Cookies 70
- Recipe 16: Air Fried Pineapple Rings 70
- Recipe 17: Air Fried Coconut Macaroons 71
- Recipe 18: Air Fried Churro Bites 71
- Recipe 19: Air Fried Strawberry Donuts 72
- Recipe 20: Air Fried S'mores Stuffed Crescent Rolls 72

CHAPTER 9: MEAL PLANNING AND PORTION CONTROL 74

- Introduction to Meal Planning and Portion Control 74
- Sample Shopping List 75

CHAPTER 10: TROUBLESHOOTING AND TIPS 77

- Common Air Frying Issues and Solutions 77
- Additional Cooking Tips and Tricks 77

CONCLUSION 78

INTRODUCTION

Diabetes is a chronic medical condition characterized by elevated levels of glucose (sugar) in the blood. This occurs when the body's ability to regulate blood sugar is impaired, typically due to issues with insulin, a hormone that helps regulate blood sugar levels. There are two main types of diabetes: Type 1, which is often diagnosed in childhood or adolescence and is primarily genetic, and Type 2, which is more commonly diagnosed in adulthood and is often associated with lifestyle factors, such as diet and exercise.

The importance of managing blood sugar levels cannot be overstated for individuals with diabetes. Uncontrolled blood sugar levels can lead to a range of serious health complications, including heart disease, kidney disease, nerve damage, vision problems, and more. Therefore, one of the key pillars of diabetes management is maintaining stable and within-target blood sugar levels.

A significant part of managing diabetes involves making healthy dietary choices. What we eat has a direct impact on our blood sugar levels, and a well-balanced diet can help keep those levels in check. This is where the concept of air frying comes into play.

Air Frying and Its Health Benefits

Air frying is a cooking method that has gained popularity in recent years, especially among those looking for healthier cooking alternatives. It involves cooking food by circulating hot air around it at a high speed, which produces a crispy, golden-brown exterior similar to frying but with significantly less oil. This cooking technique offers several health benefits that align well with the needs of individuals managing diabetes:

Reduced Oil Consumption: Traditional frying methods require a significant amount of oil, which can be high in unhealthy fats and calories. Air frying allows you to achieve the same crispy texture with a fraction of the oil or even none at all, reducing the intake of saturated fats and calories.

Lower Glycemic Index: Some foods prepared in an air fryer may have a lower glycemic index compared to their deep-fried counterparts. This means they can have a smaller impact on blood sugar levels, making them a better choice for those with diabetes.

Healthier Cooking: Air frying can help retain more nutrients in foods compared to deep frying, which often leads to nutrient loss due to prolonged exposure to high temperatures and oil.

Convenience and Versatility: Air fryers are convenient appliances that can cook a wide variety of foods, from vegetables and lean proteins to snacks and desserts. This versatility allows for a diverse and balanced diabetic-friendly diet.

In this cookbook, we will explore a range of delicious recipes specially crafted for air frying while keeping diabetes management in mind. These recipes are designed to help you enjoy tasty meals while making smart choices that support your blood sugar control and overall health.

CHAPTER 1: GETTING STARTED WITH AIR FRYING

SECTION 1.1: AN OVERVIEW OF AIR FRYERS

Air fryers have revolutionized the way we cook, offering a healthier alternative to traditional deep frying. These countertop appliances use hot air circulation to cook food to a crispy perfection. Here, we'll delve into the fundamentals of air frying and how it works:

WHAT IS AN AIR FRYER?
- An air fryer is a compact kitchen appliance designed to mimic the results of deep frying without the need for excessive oil.
- It uses a high-powered fan to circulate hot air around the food, creating a crispy exterior while retaining moisture inside.
- Air frying is an excellent option for those seeking a healthier way to enjoy their favorite fried foods.

HOW DOES AIR FRYING WORK?
- The air fryer's heating element warms the air inside the cooking chamber.
- A powerful fan distributes the hot air evenly around the food, cooking it from all sides.
- The food sits in a perforated basket or tray, allowing excess oil to drip away during cooking.
- The result is crispy and golden-brown food with less oil and fewer calories.

SECTION 1.2: TIPS FOR CHOOSING THE RIGHT AIR FRYER

Selecting the right air fryer for your needs is essential for a successful cooking experience. Here are some factors to consider when choosing an air fryer:

1. Size and Capacity:

Consider the size of your household and your cooking needs. Air fryers come in various sizes, from compact models suitable for individuals or couples to larger ones for families.

2. Wattage:

Higher wattage generally means faster and more efficient cooking. Choose a model that suits your desired cooking speed.

3. Temperature Range:

Ensure the air fryer can reach the temperatures required for the recipes you plan to cook. Most air fryers can reach up to 400°F (200°C).

4. Cooking Functions:

Some air fryers offer additional functions like baking, roasting, and grilling. Consider your cooking preferences when choosing a model.

5. Features and Accessories:

Look for air fryers with features such as digital controls, timers, and pre-set cooking programs.

Consider the availability of accessories like racks, skewers, and pans for versatile cooking options.

SECTION 1.3: BASIC OPERATING INSTRUCTIONS AND SAFETY PRECAUTIONS

Before you start air frying, it's crucial to understand how to use your appliance safely and effectively. Here are some basic operating instructions and safety precautions:

Operating Instructions:

- Place the air fryer on a flat, stable surface with ample clearance for proper air circulation.
- Preheat the air fryer as needed for your recipes; many dishes benefit from a brief preheating.
- Place your food in the cooking basket or tray, ensuring it's in a single layer for even cooking.
- Set the time and temperature according to your recipe's instructions.
- During cooking, shake or flip the food occasionally for uniform results.
- Be cautious when removing the basket or tray, as it will be hot. Use oven mitts or tongs.

Safety Precautions:

- Keep the air fryer away from flammable materials and avoid overcrowding it with food.
- Do not immerse the air fryer in water or any liquid; it's an electrical appliance.
- Ensure the appliance is unplugged when not in use, and let it cool down before storing it.
- Clean the air fryer regularly as per the manufacturer's instructions to prevent oil buildup.
- Refer to the manufacturer's user manual for specific safety guidelines and recommendations.

With these fundamental insights into air frying and proper usage, you're well-equipped to embark on a culinary journey that combines the joys of crispy, delicious food with the health-conscious choices needed to manage diabetes effectively. In the following chapters, we'll explore a variety of diabetic-friendly air fryer recipes to elevate your cooking skills.

Chapter 2: Diabetes and Nutrition

Section 2.1: How Food Affects Blood Sugar Levels

Understanding how different foods impact blood sugar levels are essential for managing diabetes effectively. Here's an explanation of how food affects blood sugar:

Carbohydrates and Blood Sugar:

- Carbohydrates are the primary nutrient that most significantly influences blood sugar levels.
- When you consume carbohydrates, your digestive system breaks them down into glucose (sugar), which enters the bloodstream.

The rate at which glucose enters the bloodstream depends on the type of carbohydrate. Simple carbohydrates, like those found in sugary snacks, because a rapid spike in blood sugar. Complex carbohydrates, found in whole grains, legumes, and vegetables, lead to a slower, steadier rise in blood sugar.

Protein and Fat:

- Protein and fat have a minimal direct impact on blood sugar levels.
- However, foods high in fat can slow down the digestion and absorption of carbohydrates, potentially leading to a delayed rise in blood sugar.

Fiber:

- Dietary fiber is a type of carbohydrate that the body cannot digest or absorb.
- Fiber helps stabilize blood sugar levels by slowing down the absorption of glucose and improving insulin sensitivity.

Section 2.2: Guidance on Carbohydrate Counting and Portion Control

For individuals with diabetes, managing carbohydrate intake is crucial. Here's some guidance on carbohydrate counting and portion control:

Carbohydrate Counting:

Carbohydrate counting involves keeping track of the grams of carbohydrates you consume in each meal or snack.It helps you better predict and control your blood sugar response to food. Consult a registered dietitian or diabetes educator to learn how to count carbs effectively and tailor it to your specific needs.

Portion Control:

- Pay attention to portion sizes to avoid overloading your body with carbohydrates.
- Use measuring cups, a food scale, or visual cues to estimate appropriate portion sizes.
- Aim for balanced meals that include a mix of carbohydrates, lean proteins, and healthy fats.

Section 2.3: The Importance of Fiber and Low Glycemic Index Foods in a Diabetic Diet

In a diabetic diet, incorporating fiber-rich foods and low glycemic index (GI) foods can help stabilize blood sugar levels and improve overall health:

Fiber:

- Foods high in fiber, such as whole grains, legumes, vegetables, and fruits, are beneficial for diabetics.
- Fiber slows the digestion and absorption of carbohydrates, preventing rapid spikes in blood sugar.
- Aim to include fiber-rich foods in your diet to promote better blood sugar control and support digestive health.

Low Glycemic Index (GI) Foods:

- The glycemic index measures how quickly a food raises blood sugar levels.
- Foods with a low GI are digested and absorbed slowly, leading to gradual increases in blood sugar.
- Prioritize low GI foods like whole grains, sweet potatoes, and non-starchy vegetables to maintain stable blood sugar levels.

Understanding the relationship between food and blood sugar levels, practicing carbohydrate counting and portion control, and incorporating fiber and low GI foods into your diet are essential components of managing diabetes through nutrition. In the following chapters, you'll find diabetic-friendly air fryer recipes that align with these dietary principles, allowing you to enjoy delicious meals while keeping your blood sugar in check.

CHAPTER 3: DIABETIC-FRIENDLY INGREDIENTS

SECTION 3.1: ESSENTIAL DIABETIC-FRIENDLY INGREDIENTS

Building a kitchen stocked with diabetic-friendly ingredients is a fundamental step in managing blood sugar levels and making healthier meals. Here's a list of essential ingredients to keep in your kitchen:

1. Whole Grains:

- Whole wheat pasta
- Brown rice
- Quinoa
- Oats

2. Lean Proteins:

- Skinless poultry (chicken, turkey)
- Lean cuts of beef and pork
- Fish (salmon, trout, tuna)
- Tofu or tempeh for vegetarian options

3. Non-Starchy Vegetables:

- Leafy greens (spinach, kale, arugula)
- Bell peppers

- Broccoli
- Cauliflower
- Zucchini
- Cucumbers

4. Legumes:

- Lentils
- Chickpeas
- Black beans
- Kidney beans

5. Healthy Fats:

- Avocado
- Olive oil (extra virgin)
- Nuts (almonds, walnuts)
- Seeds (chia seeds, flaxseeds)

6. Low-Fat Dairy or Dairy Alternatives:

- Greek yogurt (unsweetened)
- Skim or low-fat milk
- Dairy-free alternatives (almond milk, soy yogurt)

7. Herbs and Spices:

- Garlic
- Ginger
- Cinnamon
- Turmeric
- Basil
- Oregano
- Paprika
- Thyme

8. Sugar Substitutes:

- Stevia
- Erythritol
- Monk fruit
- Splenda (sucralose)
- Xylitol

9. High-Fiber Foods:

- Chia seeds
- Flaxseeds
- Psyllium husk
- Berries (blueberries, strawberries, raspberries)

Section 3.2: Sugar Substitutes and How to Use Them

Sugar substitutes are essential for diabetics who want to enjoy sweet treats without causing dramatic spikes in blood sugar. Here's an explanation of sugar substitutes and tips on how to use them:

Types of Sugar Substitutes:

- **Stevia:** Derived from the leaves of the Stevia plant, it is a natural, calorie-free sweetener.
- **Erythritol:** A sugar alcohol that has minimal impact on blood sugar and calories.
- **Monk Fruit:** Extracted from monk fruit, it is a natural, zero-calorie sweetener.
- **Splenda (Sucralose):** A synthetic sweetener with no calories.
- **Xylitol:** A sugar alcohol with a lower glycemic index than sugar but still containing some calories.

How to Use Sugar Substitutes:

- Follow package instructions for the specific sugar substitute you choose.
- Experiment to find the right sweetness level for your taste preferences.
- Be mindful that some sugar substitutes can have a cooling or bitter aftertaste when used in excess.
- Keep in mind that sugar substitutes can be significantly sweeter than sugar, so you'll need less of them.

Section 3.3: Tips for Reducing Salt and Saturated Fat in Recipes

Reducing salt and saturated fat in your cooking is important for maintaining heart health and managing diabetes. Here are some tips for doing so:

Reducing Salt:

- Use herbs, spices, and citrus zest to add flavor without relying on salt.
- Choose low-sodium or no-salt-added canned goods like tomatoes and beans.
- Limit processed and packaged foods, which often contain high levels of hidden sodium.
- Gradually reduce the amount of salt used in recipes to allow your taste buds to adjust.

Reducing Saturated Fat:

- Opt for lean cuts of meat and remove visible fat before cooking.
- Use cooking methods like grilling, baking, and air frying instead of frying in oil.
- Replace butter and lard with healthier fats like olive oil or avocado oil.
- Choose low-fat or fat-free dairy products when possible.

By incorporating these diabetic-friendly ingredients, using sugar substitutes wisely, and reducing salt and saturated fat in your recipes, you can create delicious and nutritious meals that support your blood sugar management and overall health. In the following chapters, we'll apply these principles to a range of air fryer recipes designed with diabetes in mind

Chapter 4: Breakfast Recipes

Recipe 1: Air Fried Oatmeal Pancakes
Cooking Time: 10 minutes
Servings: 2
Ingredients:
- 1 cup old-fashioned oats
- 1 ripe banana
- 1/2 cup unsweetened almond milk (or milk of your choice)
- 1 egg
- 1 teaspoon baking powder
- 1/2 teaspoon vanilla extract
- Pinch of salt
- Cooking spray or oil for the air fryer basket

Instructions:
1. In a blender or food processor, combine the oats, banana, almond milk, egg, baking powder, vanilla extract, and a pinch of salt. Blend until you have a smooth pancake batter.
2. Preheat your air fryer to 350°F (180°C) for 2 minutes.
3. Lightly grease the air fryer basket with cooking spray or oil.
4. Pour the pancake batter into the air fryer basket to form 4-inch pancakes, leaving space between them.
5. Air fry the pancakes at 350°F (180°C) for 5 minutes, or until they are golden brown on the bottom.
6. Carefully flip the pancakes using a spatula and air fry for an additional 3-4 minutes, or until the other side is golden brown and the pancakes are cooked through.
7. Serve with your choice of toppings, such as fresh berries, a dollop of Greek yogurt, or a drizzle of sugar-free syrup.

Nutrition Info (per serving):
- Calories: 235
- Carbohydrates: 42g
- Protein: 9g
- Fat: 4.5g
- Fiber: 5.5g
- Sugar: 8g

Recipe 2: Veggie and Cheese Omelette
Cooking Time: 8 minutes
Servings: 1
Ingredients:
- 2 large eggs
- 2 tablespoons low-fat shredded cheddar cheese
- 1/4 cup diced bell peppers (any color)
- 1/4 cup diced tomatoes
- 1/4 cup diced onions
- Salt and pepper to taste
- Cooking spray or oil for the air fryer basket

Instructions:
1. In a bowl, beat the eggs until well mixed. Season with a pinch of salt and pepper.
2. Preheat your air fryer to 350°F (180°C) for 2 minutes.
3. Lightly grease a heatproof dish that fits into your air fryer with cooking spray or oil.
4. Pour the beaten eggs into the dish and add the diced bell peppers, tomatoes, and onions.
5. Sprinkle the shredded cheddar cheese evenly over the top.
6. Place the dish in the air fryer basket and air fry at 350°F (180°C) for 6-8 minutes or until the omelette is set and the edges are slightly golden.
7. Carefully remove the dish from the air fryer, and using a spatula, fold the omelette in half.
8. Serve hot, garnished with additional diced veggies if desired.

Nutrition Info (per serving):
- Calories: 290
- Carbohydrates: 10g
- Protein: 21g
- Fat: 19g
- Fiber: 2g
- Sugar: 5g

RECIPE 3: GREEK YOGURT PARFAIT WITH BERRIES

Cooking Time: None
Servings: 1
Ingredients:
- 1/2 cup Greek yogurt (unsweetened)
- 1/2 cup mixed berries (e.g., strawberries, blueberries, raspberries)
- 1 tablespoon chopped nuts (e.g., almonds, walnuts)
- 1 teaspoon honey (optional for sweetness)
- 1/4 teaspoon vanilla extract (optional)

Instructions:
1. In a serving glass or bowl, start by layering half of the Greek yogurt at the bottom.
2. Add half of the mixed berries on top of the yogurt.
3. Repeat the process with the remaining yogurt and berries.
4. Sprinkle the chopped nuts over the berries.
5. If desired, drizzle a small amount of honey for added sweetness or a dash of vanilla extract for extra flavor.
6. Serve immediately or refrigerate for a healthy and satisfying breakfast or snack.

Nutrition Info (per serving, without honey):
- Calories: 195
- Carbohydrates: 16g
- Protein: 14g
- Fat: 8g
- Fiber: 3.5g
- Sugar: 10g

RECIPE 4: SPINACH AND MUSHROOM BREAKFAST QUESADILLAS

Cooking Time: 10 minutes
Servings: 2
Ingredients:

- 2 whole-grain tortillas (8-inch)
- 1 cup fresh spinach leaves
- 1/2 cup sliced mushrooms
- 1/2 cup diced bell peppers
- 2 large eggs, beaten
- 1/4 cup shredded low-fat cheese
- Salt and pepper to taste
- Cooking spray or oil for the air fryer basket

Instructions:

1. Preheat your air fryer to 350°F (180°C) for 2 minutes.
2. In a pan over medium heat, sauté the spinach, mushrooms, and bell peppers until they are tender, about 3-4 minutes. Season with a pinch of salt and pepper.
3. Lay out one tortilla on a clean surface and evenly distribute the sautéed veggies on half of the tortilla.
4. Pour the beaten eggs over the veggies and sprinkle with shredded cheese.
5. Fold the other half of the tortilla over the filling, creating a half-moon shape.
6. Lightly grease the air fryer basket with cooking spray or oil.
7. Carefully transfer the quesadilla to the air fryer basket and air fry at 350°F (180°C) for 5-6 minutes, or until the tortilla is crispy and the filling is heated through.
8. Repeat the process with the second tortilla.
9. Slice the quesadillas into wedges and serve hot.

Nutrition Info (per serving):

- Calories: 280
- Carbohydrates: 28g
- Protein: 17g
- Fat: 12g
- Fiber: 7g
- Sugar: 4g

RECIPE 5: CINNAMON APPLE RINGS

Cooking Time: 8 minutes
Servings: 2
Ingredients:

- 2 apples, cored and sliced into rings
- 1 teaspoon ground cinnamon
- 1 tablespoon powdered erythritol (or sweetener of your choice)
- Cooking spray or oil for the air fryer basket

Instructions:

1. In a bowl, mix the apple rings with ground cinnamon and powdered erythritol to coat them evenly.
2. Preheat your air fryer to 360°F (180°C) for 2 minutes.
3. Lightly grease the air fryer basket with cooking spray or oil.
4. Arrange the apple rings in a single layer in the air fryer basket.

5. Air fry at 360°F (180°C) for 4 minutes, then flip the rings and air fry for an additional 4 minutes or until they are tender and lightly browned.
6. Serve the cinnamon apple rings as a tasty and healthy breakfast or snack.

Nutrition Info (per serving):
- Calories: 90
- Carbohydrates: 24g
- Protein: 0.5g
- Fat: 0.2g
- Fiber: 4g
- Sugar: 18g

RECIPE 6: AIR FRIED BREAKFAST BURRITOS
Cooking Time: 12 minutes
Servings: 2
Ingredients:
- 2 whole wheat tortillas (8-inch)
- 4 large eggs, beaten
- 1/2 cup diced tomatoes
- 1/4 cup diced onions
- 1/4 cup diced bell peppers
- 1/4 cup shredded low-fat cheddar cheese
- Salt and pepper to taste
- Cooking spray or oil for the air fryer basket

Instructions:
- Preheat your air fryer to 350°F (180°C) for 2 minutes.
- In a bowl, beat the eggs until well mixed. Season with a pinch of salt and pepper.
- Lightly grease the air fryer basket with cooking spray or oil.
- Place one tortilla in the basket.
- Evenly distribute the diced tomatoes, onions, and bell peppers on one half of the tortilla.
- Pour the beaten eggs over the veggies and sprinkle with shredded cheese.
- Fold the other half of the tortilla over the filling, creating a half-moon shape.
- Repeat the process with the second tortilla.
- Carefully transfer both burritos to the air fryer basket and air fry at 350°F (180°C) for 8-10 minutes, or until the tortillas are crispy and the filling is heated through.
- Slice the burritos in half and serve hot.

Nutrition Info (per serving):
- Calories: 270
- Carbohydrates: 22g
- Protein: 15g
- Fat: 14g
- Fiber: 5g
- Sugar: 4g

Recipe 7: Air Fried Banana-Nut Muffins

Cooking Time: 15 minutes
Servings: 4 muffins
Ingredients:
- 2 ripe bananas, mashed
- 2 large eggs
- 1/4 cup almond flour
- 1/4 cup oat flour (gluten-free if desired)
- 1/4 cup chopped nuts (e.g., walnuts or almonds)
- 1 teaspoon baking powder
- 1/2 teaspoon ground cinnamon
- Cooking spray for the air fryer basket

Instructions:
1. Preheat your air fryer to 320°F (160°C) for 2 minutes.
2. In a mixing bowl, combine the mashed bananas and eggs until well mixed.
3. In another bowl, mix the almond flour, oat flour, chopped nuts, baking powder, and ground cinnamon.
4. Gradually add the dry ingredients to the banana and egg mixture, stirring until you have a smooth batter.
5. Lightly grease muffin cups or silicone muffin liners with cooking spray.
6. Spoon the batter into each muffin cup, filling them about two-thirds full.
7. Place the muffin cups in the air fryer basket.
8. Air fry at 320°F (160°C) for 12-15 minutes, or until the muffins are firm and a toothpick inserted into the center comes out clean.
9. Allow the muffins to cool slightly before serving.

Nutrition Info (per muffin):
- Calories: 145
- Carbohydrates: 17g
- Protein: 5g
- Fat: 7g
- Fiber: 3.5g
- Sugar: 6g

Recipe 8: Air Fried Veggie Hash Browns

Cooking Time: 15 minutes
Servings: 2
Ingredients:
- 2 medium russet potatoes, peeled and grated
- 1/2 cup diced bell peppers (any color)
- 1/4 cup diced onions
- 1/4 cup diced zucchini
- 1/4 cup diced mushrooms
- 2 tablespoons olive oil
- Salt and pepper to taste
- Cooking spray or oil for the air fryer basket

Instructions:
1. Preheat your air fryer to 375°F (190°C) for 2 minutes.

2. In a large mixing bowl, combine the grated potatoes, diced bell peppers, onions, zucchini, and mushrooms.
3. Drizzle the olive oil over the vegetable mixture and toss to coat evenly. Season with salt and pepper.
4. Lightly grease the air fryer basket with cooking spray or oil.
5. Divide the vegetable mixture into two portions and place each portion in the air fryer basket, shaping them into round patties.
6. Air fry at 375°F (190°C) for 10-12 minutes, flipping the hash browns halfway through, until they are crispy and golden brown on the outside and tender on the inside.
7. Serve the veggie hash browns as a wholesome and satisfying breakfast.

Nutrition Info (per serving):
- Calories: 220
- Carbohydrates: 33g
- Protein: 3.5g
- Fat: 9g
- Fiber: 4g
- Sugar: 4g

RECIPE 9: AIR FRIED BREAKFAST STUFFED PEPPERS

Cooking Time: 20 minutes
Servings: 2
Ingredients:
- 2 bell peppers, tops cut off and seeds removed
- 4 large eggs
- 1/4 cup diced tomatoes
- 1/4 cup diced onions
- 1/4 cup diced mushrooms
- 1/4 cup diced spinach
- 1/4 cup shredded low-fat cheddar cheese
- Salt and pepper to taste
- Cooking spray or oil for the air fryer basket

Instructions:
1. Preheat your air fryer to 350°F (180°C) for 2 minutes.
2. In a bowl, beat the eggs until well mixed. Season with a pinch of salt and pepper.
3. Lightly grease the air fryer basket with cooking spray or oil.
4. Place the bell peppers in the basket.
5. Distribute the diced tomatoes, onions, mushrooms, and spinach evenly among the bell peppers.
6. Pour the beaten eggs into each bell pepper until they are filled.
7. Sprinkle shredded cheddar cheese on top.
8. Air fry at 350°F (180°C) for 15-18 minutes, or until the eggs are set and the peppers are tender.
9. Carefully remove the stuffed peppers from the air fryer and serve hot.

Nutrition Info (per serving):
- Calories: 230
- Carbohydrates: 16g
- Protein: 15g
- Fat: 12g
- Fiber: 4g and Sugar: 8g

RECIPE 10: AIR FRIED BREAKFAST SAUSAGE AND VEGETABLE SKILLET

Cooking Time: 15 minutes
Servings: 2
Ingredients:
- 4 turkey or chicken sausage links, sliced
- 1/2 cup diced bell peppers (any color)
- 1/2 cup diced onions
- 1/2 cup diced zucchini
- 1/2 cup diced tomatoes
- 4 large eggs
- Salt and pepper to taste
- Cooking spray or oil for the air fryer basket

Instructions:
1. Preheat your air fryer to 360°F (180°C) for 2 minutes.
2. Lightly grease the air fryer basket with cooking spray or oil.
3. Add the sliced sausage links to the air fryer basket and cook at 360°F (180°C) for 5-7 minutes, or until they are heated through and slightly browned.
4. Remove the sausage from the basket and set it aside.
5. In the same greased basket, add the diced bell peppers, onions, zucchini, and tomatoes. Air fry at 360°F (180°C) for 5-7 minutes, or until the vegetables are tender and slightly caramelized.
6. Push the cooked vegetables to the sides of the basket to create a well in the center.
7. Crack the eggs into the center well, season with salt and pepper, and air fry for an additional 3-4 minutes, or until the eggs are cooked to your desired level of doneness.
8. Serve the sausage and vegetable skillet hot, with the eggs nestled among the veggies.

Nutrition Info (per serving):
- Calories: 280
- Carbohydrates: 10g
- Protein: 20g
- Fat: 18g
- Fiber: 2.5g
- Sugar: 5g

RECIPE 11: AIR FRIED BANANA AND BLUEBERRY MUFFINS

Cooking Time: 12 minutes
Servings: 4 muffins
Ingredients:
- 2 ripe bananas, mashed
- 2 large eggs
- 1/4 cup almond flour
- 1/4 cup oat flour (gluten-free if desired)
- 1/4 cup fresh blueberries
- 1/4 cup chopped nuts (e.g., walnuts or almonds)
- 1 teaspoon baking powder
- Cooking spray for the air fryer basket

Instructions:
1. Preheat your air fryer to 320°F (160°C) for 2 minutes.
2. In a mixing bowl, combine the mashed bananas and eggs until well mixed.

3. In another bowl, mix the almond flour, oat flour, blueberries, chopped nuts, and baking powder.
4. Gradually add the dry ingredients to the banana and egg mixture, stirring until you have a smooth batter.
5. Lightly grease muffin cups or silicone muffin liners with cooking spray.
6. Spoon the batter into each muffin cup, filling them about two-thirds full.
7. Place the muffin cups in the air fryer basket.
8. Air fry at 320°F (160°C) for 10-12 minutes, or until the muffins are firm and a toothpick inserted into the center comes out clean.
9. Allow the muffins to cool slightly before serving.

Nutrition Info (per muffin):
- Calories: 155
- Carbohydrates: 16g
- Protein: 5g
- Fat: 8g
- Fiber: 3g
- Sugar: 7g

RECIPE 12: AIR FRIED BREAKFAST SWEET POTATO HASH
Cooking Time: 20 minutes
Servings: 2
Ingredients:
- 2 cups sweet potatoes, peeled and diced into small cubes
- 1/2 cup diced bell peppers (any color)
- 1/2 cup diced onions
- 2 tablespoons olive oil
- 1/2 teaspoon paprika
- 1/2 teaspoon garlic powder
- Salt and pepper to taste
- Cooking spray or oil for the air fryer basket

Instructions:
1. Preheat your air fryer to 380°F (190°C) for 2 minutes.
2. In a large mixing bowl, combine the diced sweet potatoes, bell peppers, and onions.
3. Drizzle the olive oil over the vegetable mixture and toss to coat evenly. Season with paprika, garlic powder, salt, and pepper.
4. Lightly grease the air fryer basket with cooking spray or oil.
5. Place the seasoned sweet potato mixture in the air fryer basket.
6. Air fry at 380°F (190°C) for 15-18 minutes, tossing the mixture every 5 minutes, or until the sweet potatoes are crispy on the outside and tender on the inside.
7. Serve the sweet potato hash as a nutritious and flavorful breakfast side.

Nutrition Info (per serving):
- Calories: 220
- Carbohydrates: 30g
- Protein: 2g
- Fat: 10g
- Fiber: 4g
- Sugar: 7g

Recipe 13: Air Fried Cinnamon French Toast Sticks

Cooking Time: 10 minutes
Servings: 2
Ingredients:
1. 4 slices whole wheat bread, cut into sticks
2. 2 large eggs
3. 1/4 cup unsweetened almond milk (or milk of your choice)
4. 1/2 teaspoon ground cinnamon
5. 1/2 teaspoon vanilla extract
6. Cooking spray or oil for the air fryer basket
7. Sugar-free syrup for dipping (optional)

Instructions:
1. Preheat your air fryer to 350°F (180°C) for 2 minutes.
2. In a shallow bowl, whisk together the eggs, almond milk, ground cinnamon, and vanilla extract.
3. Dip each bread stick into the egg mixture, ensuring they are coated evenly.
4. Lightly grease the air fryer basket with cooking spray or oil.
5. Arrange the coated bread sticks in a single layer in the air fryer basket.
6. Air fry at 350°F (180°C) for 5-6 minutes, flipping the sticks halfway through, or until they are crispy and golden brown.
7. Serve the cinnamon French toast sticks hot, with sugar-free syrup for dipping if desired.

Nutrition Info (per serving, without syrup):
- Calories: 180
- Carbohydrates: 23g
- Protein: 9g
- Fat: 5g
- Fiber: 4g
- Sugar: 4g

Recipe 14: Air Fried Breakfast Burrito Bowl

Cooking Time: 15 minutes
Servings: 2
Ingredients:
- 2 cups cauliflower rice
- 4 large eggs
- 1/2 cup black beans, drained and rinsed
- 1/2 cup diced tomatoes
- 1/4 cup diced onions
- 1/4 cup diced bell peppers
- 1/4 cup shredded low-fat cheddar cheese
- Salt and pepper to taste
- Cooking spray or oil for the air fryer basket
- Salsa and sliced avocado for topping (optional)

Instructions:
1. Preheat your air fryer to 360°F (180°C) for 2 minutes.
2. Lightly grease the air fryer basket with cooking spray or oil.
3. Place the cauliflower rice in the basket and air fry at 360°F (180°C) for 8-10 minutes, or until it's tender and slightly crispy.

4. In a separate bowl, beat the eggs until well mixed. Season with a pinch of salt and pepper.
5. Pour the beaten eggs over the cauliflower rice in the air fryer basket.
6. Add the black beans, diced tomatoes, onions, and bell peppers to the basket.
7. Air fry at 360°F (180°C) for 5-6 minutes, stirring occasionally, until the eggs are cooked and the vegetables are heated through.
8. Sprinkle shredded cheddar cheese over the top and air fry for an additional 2 minutes, or until the cheese is melted.
9. Serve the breakfast burrito bowl hot, with optional toppings like salsa and sliced avocado.

Nutrition Info (per serving):
- Calories: 270
- Carbohydrates: 22g
- Protein: 17g
- Fat: 13g
- Fiber: 9g
- Sugar: 5g

RECIPE 15: AIR FRIED MINI FRITTATAS

Cooking Time: 12 minutes
Servings: 4 mini frittatas
Ingredients:
- 4 large eggs
- 1/4 cup diced bell peppers (any color)
- 1/4 cup diced onions
- 1/4 cup diced tomatoes
- 1/4 cup diced spinach
- 1/4 cup shredded low-fat cheddar cheese
- Salt and pepper to taste
- Cooking spray or oil for the air fryer basket

Instructions:
1. Preheat your air fryer to 350°F (180°C) for 2 minutes.
2. In a bowl, beat the eggs until well mixed. Season with a pinch of salt and pepper.
3. Lightly grease muffin cups or silicone muffin liners with cooking spray or oil.
4. Divide the diced bell peppers, onions, tomatoes, spinach, and shredded cheddar cheese evenly among the muffin cups.
5. Pour the beaten eggs over the ingredients in each muffin cup until they are filled.
6. Place the muffin cups in the air fryer basket.
7. Air fry at 350°F (180°C) for 10-12 minutes, or until the mini frittatas are set and slightly golden on top.
8. Allow the mini frittatas to cool slightly before serving.

Nutrition Info (per mini frittata):
- Calories: 80
- Carbohydrates: 2.5g
- Protein: 6g
- Fat: 5g
- Fiber: 0.5g
- Sugar: 1g

RECIPE 16: AIR FRIED AVOCADO AND EGG BREAKFAST

Cooking Time: 10 minutes
Servings: 2
Ingredients:
- 1 ripe avocado, halved and pitted
- 2 large eggs
- Salt and pepper to taste
- Fresh herbs (e.g., parsley or chives) for garnish (optional)

Instructions:
1. Preheat your air fryer to 320°F (160°C) for 2 minutes.
2. Carefully scoop out a little extra flesh from each avocado half to create a larger well for the egg.
3. Place the avocado halves in the air fryer basket.
4. Crack one egg into each avocado half, ensuring the yolk stays intact.
5. Season with salt and pepper.
6. Air fry at 320°F (160°C) for 8-10 minutes, or until the egg whites are set but the yolks are still slightly runny. Adjust the time for your desired level of doneness.
7. Garnish with fresh herbs if desired and serve hot.

Nutrition Info (per serving):
- Calories: 195
- Carbohydrates: 7g
- Protein: 6g
- Fat: 17g
- Fiber: 5g
- Sugar: 1g

RECIPE 17: AIR FRIED CINNAMON RAISIN BAGEL CHIPS

Cooking Time: 8 minutes
Servings: 2
Ingredients:
- 2 whole wheat cinnamon raisin bagels
- 1 tablespoon olive oil (or cooking spray)
- 1/2 teaspoon ground cinnamon
- Cooking spray for the air fryer basket

Instructions:
1. Preheat your air fryer to 350°F (180°C) for 2 minutes.
2. Slice the cinnamon raisin bagels into thin rounds or strips.
3. In a bowl, toss the bagel slices with olive oil (or lightly spray with cooking spray) and ground cinnamon to coat evenly.
4. Lightly grease the air fryer basket with cooking spray.
5. Arrange the bagel slices in a single layer in the air fryer basket.
6. Air fry at 350°F (180°C) for 4-5 minutes, shaking the basket or flipping the slices halfway through, until they are crispy and lightly browned.
7. Allow the cinnamon raisin bagel chips to cool slightly before serving.

Nutrition Info (per serving):
- Calories: 150
- Carbohydrates: 30g
- Protein: 4g
- Fat: 2g
- Fiber: 2g
- Sugar: 10g

RECIPE 18: AIR FRIED SPINACH AND FETA STUFFED MUSHROOMS

Cooking Time: 15 minutes
Servings: 2
Ingredients:

- 4 large mushrooms, stems removed
- 1 cup fresh spinach, chopped
- 1/4 cup crumbled feta cheese
- 1/4 cup diced onions
- 1/4 cup diced tomatoes
- 1 clove garlic, minced
- 1 teaspoon olive oil
- Salt and pepper to taste
- Cooking spray or oil for the air fryer basket

Instructions:

1. Preheat your air fryer to 360°F (180°C) for 2 minutes.
2. In a skillet, heat olive oil over medium heat. Add diced onions and minced garlic and sauté until fragrant and softened, about 2 minutes.
3. Add chopped spinach to the skillet and cook for an additional 2 minutes, or until wilted. Season with salt and pepper.
4. In a mixing bowl, combine the sautéed spinach mixture, diced tomatoes, and crumbled feta cheese. Mix well.
5. Fill each mushroom cap with the spinach and feta mixture.
6. Lightly grease the air fryer basket with cooking spray or oil.
7. Place the stuffed mushrooms in the air fryer basket.
8. Air fry at 360°F (180°C) for 10-12 minutes, or until the mushrooms are tender and the filling is heated through.
9. Serve the spinach and feta stuffed mushrooms as a savory breakfast option.

Nutrition Info (per serving):

- Calories: 80
- Carbohydrates: 7g
- Protein: 4g
- Fat: 5g
- Fiber: 2g
- Sugar: 3g

RECIPE 19: AIR FRIED BREAKFAST QUINOA BOWL

Cooking Time: 15 minutes
Servings: 2
Ingredients:

- 1 cup cooked quinoa
- 2 large eggs, scrambled
- 1/2 cup diced bell peppers (any color)
- 1/2 cup diced tomatoes
- 1/4 cup diced onions
- 1/4 cup diced avocado
- 1/4 cup shredded low-fat cheddar cheese
- Salt and pepper to taste

- Cooking spray or oil for the air fryer basket

Instructions:
1. Preheat your air fryer to 350°F (180°C) for 2 minutes.
2. In a skillet, scramble the eggs over medium heat until cooked through. Season with salt and pepper.
3. In a mixing bowl, combine the cooked quinoa, scrambled eggs, diced bell peppers, diced tomatoes, diced onions, and diced avocado. Mix well.
4. Lightly grease the air fryer basket with cooking spray or oil.
5. Place the quinoa mixture in the air fryer basket.
6. Air fry at 350°F (180°C) for 8-10 minutes, or until the quinoa is heated through and slightly crispy.
7. Sprinkle shredded cheddar cheese over the top and air fry for an additional 2 minutes, or until the cheese is melted.
8. Serve the breakfast quinoa bowl hot as a protein-packed morning meal.

Nutrition Info (per serving):
- Calories: 330
- Carbohydrates: 30g
- Protein: 15g
- Fat: 18g
- Fiber: 6g
- Sugar: 5g

RECIPE 20: AIR FRIED BREAKFAST QUICHE CUPS

Cooking Time: 15 minutes
Servings: 4 quiche cups
Ingredients:
- 4 large eggs
- 1/4 cup unsweetened almond milk (or milk of your choice)
- 1/4 cup diced bell peppers (any color)
- 1/4 cup diced onions
- 1/4 cup diced tomatoes
- 1/4 cup diced spinach
- 1/4 cup shredded low-fat cheddar cheese
- Salt and pepper to taste
- Cooking spray for the air fryer basket

Instructions:
1. Preheat your air fryer to 350°F (180°C) for 2 minutes.
2. In a bowl, whisk together the eggs and almond milk until well mixed. Season with salt and pepper.
3. Lightly grease muffin cups or silicone muffin liners with cooking spray.
4. Divide the diced bell peppers, onions, tomatoes, spinach, and shredded cheddar cheese evenly among the muffin cups.
5. Pour the egg mixture over the ingredients in each muffin cup until they are filled.
6. Place the muffin cups in the air fryer basket.
7. Air fry at 350°F (180°C) for 12-15 minutes, or until the mini quiche cups are set and slightly golden on top.
8. Allow the quiche cups to cool slightly before serving.

Nutrition Info (per quiche cup):

- Calories: 90
- Carbohydrates: 4g
- Protein: 7g
- Fat: 5g
- Fiber: 1g
- Sugar: 2g

RECIPE 21: AIR FRIED PEANUT BUTTER BANANA TOAST

Cooking Time: 5 minutes
Servings: 2
Ingredients:
- 2 slices whole wheat bread
- 2 tablespoons natural peanut butter (no added sugar)
- 1 ripe banana, sliced
- 1/2 teaspoon ground cinnamon
- Cooking spray for the air fryer basket

Instructions:
1. Preheat your air fryer to 350°F (180°C) for 2 minutes.
2. Spread 1 tablespoon of peanut butter on each slice of bread.
3. Arrange banana slices on top of the peanut butter.
4. Sprinkle ground cinnamon over the banana slices.
5. Lightly grease the air fryer basket with cooking spray.
6. Place the prepared slices of bread in the air fryer basket.
7. Air fry at 350°F (180°C) for 3-5 minutes, or until the bread is toasted, and the peanut butter is slightly melted.
8. Serve the peanut butter banana toast as a delicious and satisfying breakfast.

Nutrition Info (per serving):
- Calories: 230
- Carbohydrates: 33g
- Protein: 7g
- Fat: 9g
- Fiber: 5g
- Sugar: 11g

CHAPTER 5: APPETIZERS AND SNACKS

In this chapter, we'll explore some delightful and diabetes-friendly appetizers and snacks that you can easily prepare using your air fryer. These recipes are perfect for satisfying your cravings between meals or impressing guests with tasty starters.

RECIPE 1: CRISPY CHICKPEA SNACK
Cooking Time: 15 minutes
Servings: 4
Ingredients:
- 2 cans (15 ounces each) chickpeas, drained and rinsed
- 2 tablespoons olive oil
- 1 teaspoon ground cumin
- 1/2 teaspoon paprika
- 1/2 teaspoon garlic powder
- Salt and pepper to taste

Instructions:
1. Preheat your air fryer to 390°F (200°C) for 2 minutes.
2. In a bowl, toss the chickpeas with olive oil, ground cumin, paprika, garlic powder, salt, and pepper until they are evenly coated.
3. Lightly grease the air fryer basket with cooking spray.
4. Place the seasoned chickpeas in the air fryer basket.
5. Air fry at 390°F (200°C) for 12-15 minutes, shaking the basket or stirring the chickpeas every 5 minutes, until they are crispy and golden brown.
6. Let the crispy chickpeas cool for a few minutes before serving.

Nutrition Info (per serving):
- Calories: 190
- Carbohydrates: 28g
- Protein: 8g
- Fat: 5g
- Fiber: 7g
- Sugar: 0g

RECIPE 2: ZUCCHINI FRIES WITH YOGURT DIP
Cooking Time: 15 minutes
Servings: 4
Ingredients:
- 2 medium zucchinis, cut into fry-sized sticks
- 1/2 cup whole wheat breadcrumbs
- 1/4 cup grated Parmesan cheese
- 1 teaspoon Italian seasoning
- 1/2 teaspoon garlic powder
- 1/2 cup plain Greek yogurt
- 1 tablespoon lemon juice
- Salt and pepper to taste

- Cooking spray for the air fryer basket

Instructions:
1. Preheat your air fryer to 375°F (190°C) for 2 minutes.
2. In a bowl, combine the whole wheat breadcrumbs, grated Parmesan cheese, Italian seasoning, and garlic powder.
3. Dip the zucchini sticks into the breadcrumb mixture, ensuring they are coated evenly.
4. Lightly grease the air fryer basket with cooking spray.
5. Place the coated zucchini sticks in the air fryer basket.
6. Air fry at 375°F (190°C) for 10-12 minutes, flipping the zucchini sticks halfway through, or until they are crispy and golden brown.
7. In a separate bowl, mix the plain Greek yogurt, lemon juice, salt, and pepper to prepare the dip.
8. Serve the zucchini fries hot with the yogurt dip.

Nutrition Info (per serving with dip):
- Calories: 140
- Carbohydrates: 18g
- Protein: 9g
- Fat: 4g
- Fiber: 3g
- Sugar: 4g

RECIPE 3: GUACAMOLE-STUFFED CHERRY TOMATOES
Cooking Time: 10 minutes
Servings: 4
Ingredients:
- 16 cherry tomatoes
- 1 ripe avocado, mashed
- 1/4 cup diced red onion
- 1/4 cup diced bell pepper (any color)
- 1/4 cup chopped fresh cilantro
- 1 lime, juiced
- Salt and pepper to taste
- Cooking spray for the air fryer basket

Instructions:
1. Cut the tops off the cherry tomatoes and scoop out the seeds to create small tomato cups.
2. In a bowl, combine the mashed avocado, diced red onion, diced bell pepper, chopped cilantro, lime juice, salt, and pepper to make the guacamole.
3. Fill each cherry tomato cup with a spoonful of guacamole.
4. Lightly grease the air fryer basket with cooking spray.
5. Place the stuffed cherry tomatoes in the air fryer basket.
6. Air fry at 350°F (180°C) for 5-7 minutes, or until the cherry tomatoes are slightly softened and the guacamole is warmed.
7. Serve the guacamole-stuffed cherry tomatoes as a tasty and refreshing appetizer.

Nutrition Info (per serving):
- Calories: 75
- Carbohydrates: 6g
- Protein: 2g

- Fat: 5g
- Fiber: 3g and Sugar: 1g

RECIPE 4: AIR FRIED MOZZARELLA STICKS

Cooking Time: 10 minutes
Servings: 4
Ingredients:

- 8 mozzarella sticks, cut in half
- 1/2 cup whole wheat breadcrumbs
- 1/4 cup grated Parmesan cheese
- 1 teaspoon Italian seasoning
- 2 large eggs, beaten
- Marinara sauce for dipping (store-bought or homemade)
- Cooking spray for the air fryer basket

Instructions:

1. Preheat your air fryer to 375°F (190°C) for 2 minutes.
2. In a bowl, combine the whole wheat breadcrumbs, grated Parmesan cheese, and Italian seasoning.
3. Dip each mozzarella stick half into the beaten eggs and then into the breadcrumb mixture, coating them evenly.
4. Lightly grease the air fryer basket with cooking spray.
5. Place the coated mozzarella sticks in the air fryer basket, ensuring they are not touching.
6. Air fry at 375°F (190°C) for 6-8 minutes, or until the mozzarella sticks are crispy and the cheese is melted inside.
7. Serve the air fried mozzarella sticks hot with marinara sauce for dipping.

Nutrition Info (per serving):

- Calories: 180
- Carbohydrates: 11g
- Protein: 12g
- Fat: 10g
- Fiber: 1g
- Sugar: 1g

RECIPE 5: AIR FRIED STUFFED JALAPEÑO POPPERS

Cooking Time: 12 minutes
Servings: 4
Ingredients:

- 8 jalapeño peppers, halved and seeds removed
- 4 ounces cream cheese, softened (reduced-fat if desired)
- 1/4 cup shredded cheddar cheese (low-fat if desired)
- 2 slices turkey bacon, cooked and crumbled (optional)
- 1/2 teaspoon garlic powder
- Salt and pepper to taste
- Cooking spray for the air fryer basket

Instructions:

1. Preheat your air fryer to 375°F (190°C) for 2 minutes.
2. In a bowl, combine the softened cream cheese, shredded cheddar cheese, crumbled turkey bacon (if using), garlic powder, salt, and pepper.

3. Fill each jalapeño half with the cream cheese mixture.
4. Lightly grease the air fryer basket with cooking spray.
5. Place the stuffed jalapeño poppers in the air fryer basket.
6. Air fry at 375°F (190°C) for 10-12 minutes, or until the peppers are softened and the filling is heated through and slightly browned.
7. Serve the air fried jalapeño poppers as a spicy and creamy appetizer.

Nutrition Info (per serving):
- Calories: 120
- Carbohydrates: 3g
- Protein: 4g
- Fat: 9g
- Fiber: 1g
- Sugar: 1g

RECIPE 6: AIR FRIED SWEET POTATO FRIES WITH CHIPOTLE DIP

Cooking Time: 15 minutes
Servings: 4
Ingredients:
- 2 large sweet potatoes cut into fries
- 1 tablespoon olive oil
- 1 teaspoon smoked paprika
- 1/2 teaspoon garlic powder
- Salt and pepper to taste
- 1/2 cup plain Greek yogurt
- 1 tablespoon chipotle in adobo sauce (adjust to taste)
- Cooking spray for the air fryer basket

Instructions:
1. Preheat your air fryer to 380°F (190°C) for 2 minutes.
2. In a bowl, toss the sweet potato fries with olive oil, smoked paprika, garlic powder, salt, and pepper until they are evenly coated.
3. Lightly grease the air fryer basket with cooking spray.
4. Place the seasoned sweet potato fries in the air fryer basket.
5. Air fry at 380°F (190°C) for 12-15 minutes, shaking the basket or tossing the fries every 5 minutes, until they are crispy and golden brown.
6. While the fries are cooking, prepare the chipotle dip by mixing the plain Greek yogurt and chipotle in adobo sauce in a small bowl. Adjust the amount of chipotle to your desired level of spiciness.
7. Serve the hot and crispy sweet potato fries with the chipotle dip on the side.

Nutrition Info (per serving with dip):
- Calories: 180
- Carbohydrates: 30g
- Protein: 6g
- Fat: 5g
- Fiber: 5g
- Sugar: 7g

vvRecipe 7: Air Fried Buffalo Cauliflower Bites

Cooking Time: 15 minutes
Servings: 4
Ingredients:

- 1 small head of cauliflower, cut into bite-sized florets
- 1/2 cup whole wheat flour
- 1/2 cup water
- 1 teaspoon garlic powder
- 1/2 teaspoon smoked paprika
- 1/4 teaspoon cayenne pepper (adjust to taste)
- 1/4 cup buffalo hot sauce (sugar-free if desired)
- Cooking spray for the air fryer basket
- Ranch or blue cheese dressing for dipping (optional)

Instructions:

1. Preheat your air fryer to 380°F (190°C) for 2 minutes.
2. In a bowl, whisk together the whole wheat flour, water, garlic powder, smoked paprika, and cayenne pepper to create a batter.
3. Dip each cauliflower floret into the batter, allowing any excess to drip off, and place it in the air fryer basket.
4. Air fry at 380°F (190°C) for 12-15 minutes, flipping the cauliflower florets halfway through, or until they are crispy and golden.
5. In a separate bowl, toss the air-fried cauliflower bites with buffalo hot sauce until they are coated evenly.
6. Serve the buffalo cauliflower bites hot with ranch or blue cheese dressing for dipping, if desired.

Nutrition Info (per serving):

- Calories: 90
- Carbohydrates: 18g
- Protein: 5g
- Fat: 1g
- Fiber: 4g
- Sugar: 1g

Recipe 8: Air Fried Stuffed Mushrooms

Cooking Time: 12 minutes
Servings: 4
Ingredients:

- 16 large button mushrooms, stems removed
- 1/2 cup reduced-fat cream cheese, softened
- 2 tablespoons grated Parmesan cheese
- 2 cloves garlic, minced
- 1 tablespoon fresh parsley, chopped
- Salt and pepper to taste
- Cooking spray for the air fryer basket

Instructions:

1. Preheat your air fryer to 350°F (180°C) for 2 minutes.
2. In a bowl, mix together the softened cream cheese, grated Parmesan cheese, minced garlic, chopped parsley, salt, and pepper until well combined.

3. Fill each mushroom cap with a spoonful of the cream cheese mixture.
4. Lightly grease the air fryer basket with cooking spray.
5. Place the stuffed mushrooms in the air fryer basket.
6. Air fry at 350°F (180°C) for 10-12 minutes, or until the mushrooms are tender and the filling is lightly browned.
7. Serve the air fried stuffed mushrooms hot as a savory appetizer.

Nutrition Info (per serving):
- Calories: 70
- Carbohydrates: 3g
- Protein: 4g
- Fat: 5g
- Fiber: 1g
- Sugar: 2g

RECIPE 9: AIR FRIED CUMIN-SPICED CARROT CHIPS

Cooking Time: 15 minutes
Servings: 4
Ingredients:
- 4 large carrots, peeled and thinly sliced into rounds
- 1 tablespoon olive oil
- 1 teaspoon ground cumin
- 1/2 teaspoon ground coriander
- 1/2 teaspoon paprika
- Salt and pepper to taste
- Cooking spray for the air fryer basket

Instructions:

1. Preheat your air fryer to 380°F (190°C) for 2 minutes.
2. In a bowl, toss the carrot slices with olive oil, ground cumin, ground coriander, paprika, salt, and pepper until they are evenly coated.
3. Lightly grease the air fryer basket with cooking spray.
4. Place the seasoned carrot slices in the air fryer basket, ensuring they are in a single layer.
5. Air fry at 380°F (190°C) for 12-15 minutes, shaking the basket or tossing the slices every 5 minutes, until the carrot chips are crispy and slightly browned.
6. Let the carrot chips cool for a few minutes before serving.

Nutrition Info (per serving):

- Calories: 60
- Carbohydrates: 7g
- Protein: 1g
- Fat: 4g
- Fiber: 2g
- Sugar: 3g

RECIPE 10: AIR FRIED SPICY CAULIFLOWER BITES
Cooking Time: 15 minutes
Servings: 4
Ingredients:
- 1 medium head of cauliflower, cut into florets
- 1/2 cup whole wheat flour
- 1/2 cup water
- 1 teaspoon smoked paprika
- 1/2 teaspoon garlic powder
- 1/2 teaspoon chili powder
- 1/4 cup hot sauce (sugar-free if desired)
- Cooking spray for the air fryer basket
- Ranch or blue cheese dressing for dipping (optional)

Instructions:
1. Preheat your air fryer to 380°F (190°C) for 2 minutes.
2. In a bowl, whisk together the whole wheat flour, water, smoked paprika, garlic powder, and chili powder to create a batter.
3. Dip each cauliflower floret into the batter, allowing any excess to drip off, and place it in the air fryer basket.
4. Air fry at 380°F (190°C) for 12-15 minutes, or until the cauliflower bites are crispy and golden brown.
5. In a separate bowl, toss the air-fried cauliflower bites with hot sauce until they are coated evenly.
6. Serve the spicy cauliflower bites hot with ranch or blue cheese dressing for dipping, if desired.

Nutrition Info (per serving with dip):
- Calories: 120
- Carbohydrates: 23g
- Protein: 4g
- Fat: 1g
- Fiber: 5g
- Sugar: 3g

RECIPE 11: AIR FRIED CRISPY KALE CHIPS
Cooking Time: 10 minutes
Servings: 4
Ingredients:
- 1 bunch of kale, stems removed and leaves torn into pieces
- 1 tablespoon olive oil
- 1/2 teaspoon garlic powder
- 1/2 teaspoon paprika
- Salt and pepper to taste
- Cooking spray for the air fryer basket

Instructions:
1. Preheat your air fryer to 375°F (190°C) for 2 minutes.
2. In a bowl, toss the kale leaves with olive oil, garlic powder, paprika, salt, and pepper until they are evenly coated.
3. Lightly grease the air fryer basket with cooking spray.
4. Place the seasoned kale leaves in the air fryer basket.

5. Air fry at 375°F (190°C) for 8-10 minutes, shaking the basket or tossing the kale leaves every 3-4 minutes, until the kale chips are crispy and slightly browned.
6. Let the kale chips cool for a few minutes before serving.

Nutrition Info (per serving):
- Calories: 60
- Carbohydrates: 5g
- Protein: 2g
- Fat: 4g
- Fiber: 1g
- Sugar: 0g

RECIPE 12: AIR FRIED GARLIC PARMESAN WINGS

Cooking Time: 20 minutes
Servings: 4
Ingredients:
- 1 lb chicken wings split and tips removed
- 1/2 cup grated Parmesan cheese
- 2 teaspoons garlic powder
- 1 teaspoon dried oregano
- 1/2 teaspoon paprika
- Salt and pepper to taste
- Cooking spray for the air fryer basket

Instructions:
1. Preheat your air fryer to 375°F (190°C) for 2 minutes.
2. In a bowl, combine the grated Parmesan cheese, garlic powder, dried oregano, paprika, salt, and pepper.
3. Coat each chicken wing with the Parmesan mixture, pressing it onto the wings to adhere.
4. Lightly grease the air fryer basket with cooking spray.
5. Place the coated chicken wings in the air fryer basket in a single layer, making sure they are not touching.
6. Air fry at 375°F (190°C) for 15-18 minutes, flipping the wings halfway through, or until they are crispy and fully cooked.
7. Serve the garlic Parmesan wings hot as a flavorful appetizer.

Nutrition Info (per serving):
- Calories: 250
- Carbohydrates: 2g
- Protein: 19g
- Fat: 18g
- Fiber: 0g
- Sugar: 0g

RECIPE 13: AIR FRIED STUFFED BELL PEPPERS
Cooking Time: 18 minutes
Servings: 4
Ingredients:
- 4 bell peppers, any color
- 1/2 lb lean ground turkey or chicken
- 1/2 cup cooked quinoa
- 1/4 cup diced tomatoes
- 1/4 cup diced onions
- 1/4 cup shredded low-fat cheddar cheese
- 1/4 teaspoon garlic powder
- Salt and pepper to taste
- Cooking spray for the air fryer basket

Instructions:
1. Preheat your air fryer to 350°F (180°C) for 2 minutes.
2. Cut the tops off the bell peppers and remove the seeds.
3. In a skillet, cook the ground turkey or chicken over medium heat until browned. Drain any excess fat.
4. In a bowl, mix the cooked turkey or chicken, cooked quinoa, diced tomatoes, diced onions, shredded cheddar cheese, garlic powder, salt, and pepper.
5. Stuff each bell pepper with the mixture.
6. Lightly grease the air fryer basket with cooking spray.
7. Place the stuffed bell peppers in the air fryer basket.
8. Air fry at 350°F (180°C) for 15-18 minutes, or until the peppers are tender and the filling is heated through.
9. Serve the air fried stuffed bell peppers as a delicious and satisfying snack or appetizer.

Nutrition Info (per serving):
- Calories: 190
- Carbohydrates: 15g
- Protein: 17g
- Fat: 7g
- Fiber: 3g
- Sugar: 5g

RECIPE 14: AIR FRIED CINNAMON APPLE CHIPS
Cooking Time: 10 minutes
Servings: 4
Ingredients:
- 2 apples, thinly sliced
- 1 tablespoon cinnamon
- 1 tablespoon granulated sweetener (e.g., Stevia, Erythritol)
- Cooking spray for the air fryer basket

Instructions:
1. Preheat your air fryer to 350°F (180°C) for 2 minutes.
2. In a bowl, toss the apple slices with cinnamon and granulated sweetener until they are evenly coated.
3. Lightly grease the air fryer basket with cooking spray.

4. Place the coated apple slices in the air fryer basket in a single layer.
5. Air fry at 350°F (180°C) for 5-7 minutes, flipping the apple slices halfway through, or until they are crispy and slightly browned.
6. Let the cinnamon apple chips cool for a few minutes before serving.

Nutrition Info (per serving):
- Calories: 70
- Carbohydrates: 19g
- Protein: 0g
- Fat: 0g
- Fiber: 4g
- Sugar: 14g

RECIPE 15: AIR FRIED STUFFED JALAPEÑO MUSHROOMS

Cooking Time: 15 minutes
Servings: 4
Ingredients:
1. 8 large white button mushrooms, stems removed
2. 4 jalapeño peppers, halved and seeds removed
3. 1/2 cup reduced-fat cream cheese, softened
4. 1/4 cup shredded cheddar cheese (low-fat if desired)
5. 2 cloves garlic, minced
6. Salt and pepper to taste
7. Cooking spray for the air fryer basket

Instructions:
1. Preheat your air fryer to 350°F (180°C) for 2 minutes.
2. In a bowl, mix together the softened cream cheese, shredded cheddar cheese, minced garlic, salt, and pepper.
3. Fill each mushroom cap with a spoonful of the cream cheese mixture.
4. Stuff each halved jalapeño pepper with a stuffed mushroom.
5. Lightly grease the air fryer basket with cooking spray.
6. Place the stuffed jalapeño mushrooms in the air fryer basket.
7. Air fry at 350°F (180°C) for 10-12 minutes, or until the mushrooms are tender, the jalapeños are slightly softened, and the filling is heated through.
8. Serve the air fried stuffed jalapeño mushrooms as a delicious and mildly spicy appetizer.

Nutrition Info (per serving):
- Calories: 80
- Carbohydrates: 6g
- Protein: 4g
- Fat: 5g
- Fiber: 1g
- Sugar: 2g

Recipe 16: Air Fried Avocado Fries

Cooking Time: 10 minutes
Servings: 4
Ingredients:
- 2 ripe avocados, sliced into thick strips
- 1 cup whole wheat breadcrumbs
- 2 eggs, beaten
- 1/2 teaspoon paprika
- 1/2 teaspoon garlic powder
- Salt and pepper to taste
- Cooking spray for the air fryer basket
- Salsa or dipping sauce of your choice (optional)

Instructions:
1. Preheat your air fryer to 375°F (190°C) for 2 minutes.
2. In a bowl, combine the whole wheat breadcrumbs, paprika, garlic powder, salt, and pepper.
3. Dip each avocado strip into the beaten eggs and then into the breadcrumb mixture, coating them evenly.
4. Lightly grease the air fryer basket with cooking spray.
5. Place the coated avocado strips in the air fryer basket.
6. Air fry at 375°F (190°C) for 5-7 minutes, or until the avocado fries are crispy and lightly browned.
7. Serve the air fried avocado fries hot with salsa or your favorite dipping sauce, if desired.

Nutrition Info (per serving):
- Calories: 210
- Carbohydrates: 21g
- Protein: 7g
- Fat: 12g
- Fiber: 8g
- Sugar: 2g

Recipe 17: Air Fried Cajun Spiced Pecans

Cooking Time: 8 minutes
Servings: 4
Ingredients:
- 2 cups pecan halves
- 1 tablespoon olive oil
- 1 teaspoon Cajun seasoning (adjust to taste)
- 1/2 teaspoon paprika
- 1/2 teaspoon garlic powder
- Salt to taste

Instructions:
1. Preheat your air fryer to 350°F (180°C) for 2 minutes.
2. In a bowl, toss the pecan halves with olive oil, Cajun seasoning, paprika, garlic powder, and salt until they are evenly coated.
3. Lightly grease the air fryer basket with cooking spray.
4. Place the seasoned pecans in the air fryer basket in a single layer.
5. Air fry at 350°F (180°C) for 6-8 minutes, shaking the basket or stirring the pecans every 2 minutes, until the pecans are toasted and fragrant.

6. Let the Cajun spiced pecans cool for a few minutes before serving.

Nutrition Info (per serving):
- Calories: 220
- Carbohydrates: 5g
- Protein: 3g
- Fat: 23g
- Fiber: 4g
- Sugar: 1g

RECIPE 18: AIR FRIED MINI CAPRESE SKEWERS
Cooking Time: 8 minutes
Servings: 4
Ingredients:
- 16 cherry tomatoes
- 16 fresh mozzarella balls (bocconcini)
- 16 fresh basil leaves
- 2 tablespoons balsamic glaze
- Salt and pepper to taste
- Wooden toothpicks

Instructions:
1. Preheat your air fryer to 350°F (180°C) for 2 minutes.
2. Assemble the mini Caprese skewers by threading a cherry tomato, a mozzarella ball, and a basil leaf onto each wooden toothpick, repeating until you have 16 skewers.
3. Lightly grease the air fryer basket with cooking spray.
4. Place the assembled skewers in the air fryer basket.
5. Air fry at 350°F (180°C) for 6-8 minutes, or until the mozzarella balls are slightly melted and the tomatoes are warmed.
6. Drizzle the balsamic glaze over the skewers and season with salt and pepper to taste.
7. Serve the mini Caprese skewers as a refreshing and elegant appetizer.

Nutrition Info (per serving):
- Calories: 90
- Carbohydrates: 5g
- Protein: 6g
- Fat: 5g
- Fiber: 1g
- Sugar: 3g

RECIPE 19: AIR FRIED EDAMAME WITH SEA SALT
Cooking Time: 10 minutes
Servings: 4
Ingredients:
- 2 cups frozen edamame (unshelled)
- 1 tablespoon olive oil
- Sea salt to taste

Instructions:
1. Preheat your air fryer to 375°F (190°C) for 2 minutes.
2. In a bowl, toss the frozen edamame with olive oil until they are evenly coated.

3. Lightly grease the air fryer basket with cooking spray.
4. Place the edamame in the air fryer basket.
5. Air fry at 375°F (190°C) for 8-10 minutes, shaking the basket or tossing the edamame every 3-4 minutes, until they are heated through and slightly crispy.
6. Season the air fried edamame with sea salt to taste.
7. Serve the edamame as a nutritious and crunchy snack.

Nutrition Info (per serving):
- Calories: 120
- Carbohydrates: 7g
- Protein: 7g
- Fat: 6g
- Fiber: 4g
- Sugar: 1g

RECIPE 20: AIR FRIED BUFFALO CAULIFLOWER BITES
Cooking Time: 15 minutes
Servings: 4
Ingredients:
- 1 small head of cauliflower, cut into florets
- 1/2 cup whole wheat flour
- 1/2 cup water
- 1 teaspoon garlic powder
- 1/2 teaspoon smoked paprika
- 1/4 teaspoon cayenne pepper (adjust to taste)
- 1/4 cup buffalo hot sauce (sugar-free if desired)
- Cooking spray for the air fryer basket
- Ranch or blue cheese dressing for dipping (optional)

Instructions:
1. Preheat your air fryer to 375°F (190°C) for 2 minutes.
2. In a bowl, whisk together the whole wheat flour, water, garlic powder, smoked paprika, and cayenne pepper to create a batter.
3. Dip each cauliflower floret into the batter, allowing any excess to drip off, and place it in the air fryer basket.
4. Air fry at 375°F (190°C) for 12-15 minutes, flipping the cauliflower florets halfway through, or until they are crispy and golden brown.
5. In a separate bowl, toss the air-fried cauliflower bites with buffalo hot sauce until they are coated evenly.
6. Serve the buffalo cauliflower bites hot with ranch or blue cheese dressing for dipping, if desired.

Nutrition Info (per serving with dip):
- Calories: 120
- Carbohydrates: 23g
- Protein: 4g
- Fat: 1g
- Fiber: 5g
- Sugar: 3g

RECIPE 21: AIR FRIED COCONUT SHRIMP

Cooking Time: 12 minutes
Servings: 4
Ingredients:
- 1 lb large shrimp, peeled and deveined
- 1/2 cup shredded coconut
- 1/2 cup whole wheat breadcrumbs
- 2 large eggs, beaten
- Cooking spray for the air fryer basket
- Sweet chili sauce for dipping (optional)

Instructions:
1. Preheat your air fryer to 375°F (190°C) for 2 minutes.
2. In a bowl, combine the shredded coconut and whole wheat breadcrumbs.
3. Dip each shrimp into the beaten eggs and then into the coconut breadcrumb mixture, pressing it onto the shrimp to adhere.
4. Lightly grease the air fryer basket with cooking spray.
5. Place the coated shrimp in the air fryer basket in a single layer.
6. Air fry at 375°F (190°C) for 10-12 minutes, flipping the shrimp halfway through, or until they are crispy and golden brown.
7. Serve the air fried coconut shrimp hot with sweet chili sauce for dipping, if desired.

Nutrition Info (per serving with dip):
- Calories: 220
- Carbohydrates: 17g
- Protein: 15g
- Fat: 10g
- Fiber: 3g
- Sugar: 4g

Chapter 6: Main Courses

Recipe 1: Lemon Herb Chicken Thighs
Cooking Time: 25 minutes
Servings: 4
Ingredients:
- 4 bone-in, skin-on chicken thighs
- 2 tablespoons olive oil
- 2 cloves garlic, minced
- 1 lemon, zested and juiced
- 1 teaspoon dried oregano
- 1 teaspoon dried thyme
- Salt and pepper to taste
- Lemon wedges for garnish (optional)

Instructions:
1. Preheat your air fryer to 375°F (190°C) for 2 minutes.
2. In a bowl, combine the olive oil, minced garlic, lemon zest, lemon juice, dried oregano, dried thyme, salt, and pepper.
3. Pat the chicken thighs dry with paper towels.
4. Brush the chicken thighs with the lemon herb mixture, ensuring they are evenly coated.
5. Place the chicken thighs in the air fryer basket, skin-side down.
6. Air fry at 375°F (190°C) for 15 minutes, then flip the chicken thighs and air fry for an additional 10 minutes, or until they are cooked through and the skin is crispy.
7. Garnish with lemon wedges if desired and serve the lemon herb chicken thighs hot.

Nutrition Info (per serving):
- Calories: 320
- Carbohydrates: 2g
- Protein: 22g
- Fat: 24g
- Fiber: 1g
- Sugar: 0g

Recipe 2: Balsamic Glazed Salmon
Cooking Time: 12 minutes
Servings: 4
Ingredients:
- 4 salmon fillets (6 oz each)
- 1/4 cup balsamic vinegar
- 2 tablespoons olive oil
- 2 cloves garlic, minced
- 2 tablespoons honey (or a sugar-free sweetener)
- Salt and pepper to taste
- Fresh chopped parsley for garnish (optional)

Instructions:
1. Preheat your air fryer to 375°F (190°C) for 2 minutes.
2. In a bowl, whisk together the balsamic vinegar, olive oil, minced garlic, honey, salt, and pepper to create the glaze.

3. Place the salmon fillets in a shallow dish and pour half of the balsamic glaze over them. Let them marinate for 10 minutes.
4. Lightly grease the air fryer basket with cooking spray.
5. Place the marinated salmon fillets in the air fryer basket.
6. Air fry at 375°F (190°C) for 10-12 minutes, brushing the fillets with the remaining glaze halfway through, or until the salmon is flaky and cooked to your desired level of doneness.
7. Garnish with fresh chopped parsley if desired and serve the balsamic glazed salmon hot.

Nutrition Info (per serving):
- Calories: 330
- Carbohydrates: 10g
- Protein: 30g
- Fat: 18g
- Fiber: 0g
- Sugar: 9g

RECIPE 3: TURKEY AND VEGETABLE STUFFED BELL PEPPERS
Cooking Time: 20 minutes
Servings: 4
Ingredients:
- 4 large bell peppers, any color
- 1 lb lean ground turkey
- 1 cup cooked quinoa
- 1/2 cup diced tomatoes
- 1/2 cup diced onions
- 1/2 cup diced zucchini
- 1/2 cup shredded low-fat mozzarella cheese
- 1/2 teaspoon garlic powder
- Salt and pepper to taste
- Cooking spray for the air fryer basket

Instructions:
1. Preheat your air fryer to 350°F (180°C) for 2 minutes.
2. Cut the tops off the bell peppers and remove the seeds.
3. In a skillet, cook the ground turkey over medium heat until browned. Drain any excess fat.
4. In a bowl, mix the cooked turkey, cooked quinoa, diced tomatoes, diced onions, diced zucchini, shredded mozzarella cheese, garlic powder, salt, and pepper.
5. Stuff each bell pepper with the turkey and vegetable mixture.
6. Lightly grease the air fryer basket with cooking spray.
7. Place the stuffed bell peppers in the air fryer basket.
8. Air fry at 350°F (180°C) for 18-20 minutes, or until the peppers are tender and the filling is heated through.
9. Serve the turkey and vegetable stuffed bell peppers hot as a nutritious main course.

Nutrition Info (per serving):
- Calories: 330
- Carbohydrates: 31g
- Protein: 31g
- Fat: 10g
- Fiber: 6g
- Sugar: 8g

RECIPE 4: AIR FRIED SHRIMP SCAMPI

Cooking Time: 10 minutes
Servings: 4
Ingredients:
- 1 lb large shrimp, peeled and deveined
- 3 tablespoons melted butter
- 4 cloves garlic, minced
- 1/4 teaspoon red pepper flakes (optional)
- Zest and juice of 1 lemon
- Salt and black pepper to taste
- Chopped fresh parsley for garnish

Instructions:
1. Preheat your air fryer to 375°F (190°C) for 2 minutes.
2. In a bowl, combine the melted butter, minced garlic, red pepper flakes (if using), lemon zest, and lemon juice.
3. Toss the shrimp in the butter mixture until they are evenly coated.
4. Place the shrimp in the air fryer basket in a single layer.
5. Air fry at 375°F (190°C) for 5-7 minutes, shaking the basket halfway through, or until the shrimp are pink and cooked through.
6. Season with salt and black pepper to taste, garnish with chopped fresh parsley, and serve the shrimp scampi hot.

Nutrition Info (per serving):
- Calories: 180
- Carbohydrates: 2g
- Protein: 24g
- Fat: 8g
- Fiber: 0g
- Sugar: 0g

RECIPE 5: AIR FRIED TERIYAKI TOFU STIR FRY

Cooking Time: 15 minutes
Servings: 4
Ingredients:
- 1 block firm tofu, pressed and cubed
- 1/4 cup low-sodium soy sauce
- 2 tablespoons honey (or a sugar-free sweetener)
- 1 tablespoon rice vinegar
- 2 cloves garlic, minced
- 1 teaspoon grated ginger
- 1 tablespoon cornstarch
- 1 tablespoon water
- 2 cups mixed vegetables (such as bell peppers, broccoli, carrots), chopped
- Cooked brown rice for serving

Instructions:
1. Preheat your air fryer to 375°F (190°C) for 2 minutes.
2. In a bowl, whisk together the soy sauce, honey, rice vinegar, minced garlic, and grated ginger.
3. In a separate small bowl, mix the cornstarch and water to create a slurry.

4. Toss the tofu cubes in the soy sauce mixture until they are well coated. Then, toss them in the cornstarch slurry.
5. Place the coated tofu in the air fryer basket and air fry at 375°F (190°C) for 10-12 minutes, shaking the basket halfway through, or until the tofu is crispy and golden brown.
6. In the last 5 minutes of air frying, add the mixed vegetables to the air fryer basket and stir to combine. Continue air frying until the vegetables are tender-crisp.
7. Serve the teriyaki tofu and vegetables over cooked brown rice.

Nutrition Info (per serving, excluding rice):
- Calories: 180
- Carbohydrates: 16g
- Protein: 14g
- Fat: 8g
- Fiber: 3g
- Sugar: 9g

RECIPE 6: AIR FRIED BEEF AND BROCCOLI

Cooking Time: 12 minutes
Servings: 4
Ingredients:
- 1 lb lean beef steak (such as sirloin), thinly sliced
- 2 cups broccoli florets
- 2 cloves garlic, minced
- 1/4 cup low-sodium soy sauce
- 2 tablespoons hoisin sauce
- 1 tablespoon honey (or a sugar-free sweetener)
- 1 tablespoon cornstarch
- 1 tablespoon water
- Sesame seeds and sliced green onions for garnish (optional)
- Cooked brown rice for serving

Instructions:
1. Preheat your air fryer to 375°F (190°C) for 2 minutes.
2. In a bowl, whisk together the soy sauce, hoisin sauce, honey, and minced garlic.
3. In a separate small bowl, mix the cornstarch and water to create a slurry.
4. Toss the thinly sliced beef in the soy sauce mixture until it's well coated. Then, toss it in the cornstarch slurry.
5. Place the coated beef slices in the air fryer basket in a single layer.
6. Air fry at 375°F (190°C) for 8-10 minutes, shaking the basket halfway through, or until the beef is browned and cooked to your desired level of doneness.
7. In the last 5 minutes of air frying, add the broccoli florets to the air fryer basket and stir to combine. Continue air frying until the broccoli is tender-crisp.
8. Serve the beef and broccoli over cooked brown rice, garnished with sesame seeds and sliced green onions if desired.

Nutrition Info (per serving, excluding rice):
- Calories: 240
- Carbohydrates: 15g
- Protein: 25g
- Fat: 9g
- Fiber: 2g
- Sugar: 7g

Recipe 7: Air Fried BBQ Pulled Pork Sandwiches

Cooking Time: 15 minutes
Servings: 4
Ingredients:
- 1 lb pulled pork (cooked and shredded)
- 1/2 cup barbecue sauce (sugar-free if desired)
- 4 whole wheat hamburger buns
- Coleslaw (store-bought or homemade) for topping
- Sliced pickles for garnish (optional)

Instructions:
1. Preheat your air fryer to 375°F (190°C) for 2 minutes.
2. In a bowl, mix the pulled pork and barbecue sauce until the pork is evenly coated.
3. Lightly toast the whole wheat hamburger buns in the air fryer for 1-2 minutes.
4. Place the sauced pulled pork in the air fryer basket.
5. Air fry at 375°F (190°C) for 8-10 minutes, stirring occasionally, or until the pork is heated through and slightly crispy.
6. Assemble the pulled pork sandwiches by placing the sauced pork on the toasted buns and topping with coleslaw and sliced pickles if desired.
7. Serve the BBQ pulled pork sandwiches hot.

Nutrition Info (per serving):
- Calories: 450
- Carbohydrates: 45g
- Protein: 25g
- Fat: 18g
- Fiber: 5g
- Sugar: 11g

Recipe 8: Air Fried Vegetable Stir-Fry

Cooking Time: 10 minutes
Servings: 4
Ingredients:
- 2 cups mixed vegetables (such as bell peppers, broccoli, carrots, snap peas), chopped
- 1 tablespoon low-sodium soy sauce
- 1 tablespoon hoisin sauce
- 1 teaspoon sesame oil
- 1 clove garlic, minced
- 1/2 teaspoon grated ginger
- Cooked brown rice for serving

Instructions:
1. Preheat your air fryer to 375°F (190°C) for 2 minutes.
2. In a bowl, whisk together the soy sauce, hoisin sauce, sesame oil, minced garlic, and grated ginger.
3. Toss the chopped vegetables in the sauce mixture until they are well coated.
4. Place the coated vegetables in the air fryer basket in a single layer.
5. Air fry at 375°F (190°C) for 7-9 minutes, shaking the basket halfway through, or until the vegetables are tender-crisp.
6. Serve the air fried vegetable stir-fry over cooked brown rice.

Nutrition Info (per serving, excluding rice):
- Calories: 70
- Carbohydrates: 13g
- Protein: 2g
- Fat: 2g
- Fiber: 3g
- Sugar: 4g

RECIPE 9: AIR FRIED VEGETARIAN QUESADILLAS

Cooking Time: 10 minutes
Servings: 4
Ingredients:
- 4 whole wheat tortillas
- 1 cup shredded low-fat cheddar cheese
- 1 cup black beans, drained and rinsed
- 1 cup corn kernels (fresh, frozen, or canned)
- 1/2 cup diced bell peppers
- 1/2 cup diced red onion
- 1/2 teaspoon ground cumin
- Cooking spray for the air fryer basket
- Salsa and Greek yogurt (as toppings, optional)

Instructions:
1. Preheat your air fryer to 375°F (190°C) for 2 minutes.
2. In a bowl, combine the black beans, corn, diced bell peppers, diced red onion, and ground cumin.
3. Lay one tortilla flat and sprinkle a quarter of the shredded cheddar cheese evenly over half of it.
4. Spoon a quarter of the bean and vegetable mixture over the cheese.
5. Fold the tortilla in half to create a quesadilla.
6. Repeat steps 3-5 with the remaining tortillas and fillings.
7. Lightly grease the air fryer basket with cooking spray.
8. Place the quesadillas in the air fryer basket, ensuring they are not overlapping.
9. Air fry at 375°F (190°C) for 5 minutes, carefully flip the quesadillas, and air fry for an additional 3-5 minutes, or until they are crispy and the cheese is melted.
10. Serve the vegetarian quesadillas hot with salsa and Greek yogurt, if desired.

Nutrition Info (per serving, without toppings):
- Calories: 280
- Carbohydrates: 45g
- Protein: 15g
- Fat: 5g
- Fiber: 10g
- Sugar: 4g

RECIPE 10: AIR FRIED SPICY TOFU AND VEGETABLE SKEWERS

Cooking Time: 15 minutes
Servings: 4
Ingredients:
- 1 block extra-firm tofu, cubed
- 2 cups mixed vegetables (such as bell peppers, zucchini, cherry tomatoes), cut into chunks
- 2 tablespoons olive oil
- 1 tablespoon sriracha sauce (adjust to taste)
- 1 teaspoon smoked paprika
- 1/2 teaspoon garlic powder
- Salt and pepper to taste
- Wooden skewers, soaked in water

Instructions:
1. Preheat your air fryer to 375°F (190°C) for 2 minutes.
2. In a bowl, whisk together the olive oil, sriracha sauce, smoked paprika, garlic powder, salt, and pepper.
3. Thread the cubed tofu and mixed vegetables onto the wooden skewers, alternating between tofu and vegetables.
4. Brush the skewers with the spicy olive oil mixture until they are well coated.
5. Place the skewers in the air fryer basket.
6. Air fry at 375°F (190°C) for 12-15 minutes, turning the skewers occasionally, or until the tofu is crispy and the vegetables are tender.
7. Serve the spicy tofu and vegetable skewers hot.

Nutrition Info (per serving):
- Calories: 220
- Carbohydrates: 10g
- Protein: 14g
- Fat: 15g
- Fiber: 3g
- Sugar: 4g

RECIPE 11: AIR FRIED STUFFED PORTOBELLO MUSHROOMS

Cooking Time: 15 minutes
Servings: 4
Ingredients:
- 4 large Portobello mushrooms, stems removed and gills scraped
- 1 cup spinach, chopped
- 1/2 cup diced red bell pepper
- 1/2 cup diced onion
- 1/2 cup crumbled feta cheese
- 2 cloves garlic, minced
- 2 tablespoons olive oil
- Salt and pepper to taste

Instructions:
1. Preheat your air fryer to 375°F (190°C) for 2 minutes.
2. In a skillet, heat the olive oil over medium heat. Add the diced onion and red bell pepper and sauté for 3-4 minutes, or until softened.

3. Add the minced garlic and chopped spinach to the skillet. Sauté for an additional 2 minutes until the spinach wilts. Season with salt and pepper.
4. Remove the skillet from heat and stir in the crumbled feta cheese.
5. Stuff each Portobello mushroom cap with the spinach, onion, pepper, and feta mixture.
6. Place the stuffed mushrooms in the air fryer basket.
7. Air fry at 375°F (190°C) for 12-15 minutes, or until the mushrooms are tender and the filling is heated through.
8. Serve the stuffed Portobello mushrooms hot as a flavorful main course.

Nutrition Info (per serving):
- Calories: 180
- Carbohydrates: 10g
- Protein: 8g
- Fat: 13g
- Fiber: 3g
- Sugar: 4g

RECIPE 12: AIR FRIED CAJUN SHRIMP AND SAUSAGE SKILLET

Cooking Time: 12 minutes
Servings: 4
Ingredients:
- 1 lb large shrimp, peeled and deveined
- 8 oz Andouille sausage, sliced
- 2 cups bell peppers (a mix of red, yellow, and green), sliced
- 1 cup diced tomatoes (canned or fresh)
- 1 tablespoon olive oil
- 1 tablespoon Cajun seasoning
- Salt and pepper to taste
- Cooked rice or cauliflower rice for serving

Instructions:
1. Preheat your air fryer to 375°F (190°C) for 2 minutes.
2. In a bowl, toss the shrimp and Andouille sausage with the olive oil and Cajun seasoning until they are well coated.
3. Place the seasoned shrimp and sausage in the air fryer basket.
4. Air fry at 375°F (190°C) for 8-10 minutes, shaking the basket halfway through, or until the shrimp are pink and cooked through.
5. In a separate skillet, sauté the sliced bell peppers until they are slightly softened.
6. Add the diced tomatoes to the skillet and heat through.
7. Serve the Cajun shrimp and sausage over cooked rice or cauliflower rice, topped with the sautéed bell peppers and tomatoes.

Nutrition Info (per serving, excluding rice):
- Calories: 280
- Carbohydrates: 9g
- Protein: 25g
- Fat: 16g
- Fiber: 3g
- Sugar: 5g

Recipe 13: Air Fried Stuffed Chicken Breasts
Cooking Time: 25 minutes
Servings: 4
Ingredients:
- 4 boneless, skinless chicken breasts
- 1 cup baby spinach
- 1/2 cup low-fat ricotta cheese
- 1/4 cup sun-dried tomatoes, chopped
- 2 cloves garlic, minced
- 1/4 cup grated Parmesan cheese
- Salt and pepper to taste
- Cooking spray for the air fryer basket

Instructions:
1. Preheat your air fryer to 375°F (190°C) for 2 minutes.
2. In a bowl, combine the baby spinach, low-fat ricotta cheese, chopped sun-dried tomatoes, minced garlic, grated Parmesan cheese, salt, and pepper.
3. Make a horizontal slit in each chicken breast to create a pocket.
4. Stuff each chicken breast with the spinach and ricotta mixture, pressing it down gently.
5. Lightly grease the air fryer basket with cooking spray.
6. Place the stuffed chicken breasts in the air fryer basket.
7. Air fry at 375°F (190°C) for 20-25 minutes, or until the chicken is cooked through and no longer pink in the center.
8. Serve the stuffed chicken breasts hot as a delicious main course.

Nutrition Info (per serving):
- Calories: 250
- Carbohydrates: 6g
- Protein: 38g
- Fat: 8g
- Fiber: 2g
- Sugar: 2g

Recipe 14: Air Fried Eggplant Parmesan
Cooking Time: 20 minutes
Servings: 4
Ingredients:
- 2 medium eggplants, sliced into 1/2-inch rounds
- 2 cups marinara sauce (store-bought or homemade)
- 1 1/2 cups shredded mozzarella cheese
- 1/2 cup grated Parmesan cheese
- 1/2 cup breadcrumbs (whole wheat for a healthier option)
- 1/4 cup chopped fresh basil leaves
- Cooking spray for the air fryer basket

Instructions:
1. Preheat your air fryer to 375°F (190°C) for 2 minutes.
2. In a bowl, combine the breadcrumbs and grated Parmesan cheese.
3. Dip each eggplant slice into the breadcrumb mixture, pressing it down to adhere, and place it in the air fryer basket.

4. Lightly grease the air fryer basket with cooking spray.
5. Air fry the breaded eggplant slices at 375°F (190°C) for 10-12 minutes, flipping them halfway through, or until they are golden brown and crispy.
6. In an oven-safe dish, layer marinara sauce, air-fried eggplant slices, shredded mozzarella cheese, and chopped basil leaves. Repeat the layers.
7. Air fry the assembled dish at 375°F (190°C) for an additional 5-8 minutes, or until the cheese is melted and bubbly.
8. Serve the air fried eggplant Parmesan hot as a hearty main course.

Nutrition Info (per serving):
- Calories: 350
- Carbohydrates: 29g
- Protein: 18g
- Fat: 18g
- Fiber: 9g
- Sugar: 10g

RECIPE 15: AIR FRIED PORK TENDERLOIN WITH APPLE COMPOTE

Cooking Time: 20 minutes
Servings: 4
Ingredients:
- 1 lb pork tenderloin
- 2 tablespoons olive oil
- 1 teaspoon dried rosemary
- Salt and pepper to taste

For the Apple Compote:
- 2 apples, peeled, cored, and chopped
- 1/4 cup water
- 2 tablespoons honey (or a sugar-free sweetener)
- 1/2 teaspoon cinnamon
- 1/4 teaspoon nutmeg

Instructions:
1. Preheat your air fryer to 375°F (190°C) for 2 minutes.
2. Rub the pork tenderloin with olive oil and season it with dried rosemary, salt, and pepper.
3. Place the pork tenderloin in the air fryer basket.
4. Air fry at 375°F (190°C) for 18-20 minutes, turning the tenderloin halfway through, or until it reaches an internal temperature of 145°F (63°C).
5. While the pork is cooking, prepare the apple compote. In a saucepan, combine the chopped apples, water, honey, cinnamon, and nutmeg. Simmer over medium heat until the apples are soft and the mixture thickens, about 10 minutes.
6. Slice the cooked pork tenderloin and serve it with the warm apple compote.

Nutrition Info (per serving, excluding apple compote):
- Calories: 180
- Carbohydrates: 0g
- Protein: 24g
- Fat: 9g
- Fiber: 0g

- Sugar: 0g

RECIPE 16: AIR FRIED THAI BASIL TOFU STIR-FRY
Cooking Time: 15 minutes
Servings: 4
Ingredients:
- 1 block extra-firm tofu, cubed
- 2 cups mixed bell peppers, sliced
- 1 cup sliced snap peas
- 1/2 cup sliced carrots
- 2 cloves garlic, minced
- 2 tablespoons soy sauce
- 1 tablespoon oyster sauce (or hoisin sauce for a vegetarian option)
- 1 tablespoon fresh basil leaves, chopped
- 1/2 teaspoon red pepper flakes (adjust to taste)
- Cooking spray for the air fryer basket
- Cooked jasmine rice for serving

Instructions:
1. Preheat your air fryer to 375°F (190°C) for 2 minutes.
2. In a bowl, mix the cubed tofu, minced garlic, soy sauce, oyster sauce (or hoisin sauce), and red pepper flakes.
3. Lightly grease the air fryer basket with cooking spray.
4. Place the tofu cubes in the air fryer basket.
5. Air fry at 375°F (190°C) for 10-12 minutes, shaking the basket halfway through, or until the tofu is crispy and golden.
6. In the last 5 minutes of air frying, add the sliced bell peppers, snap peas, and carrots to the air fryer basket and stir to combine. Continue air frying until the vegetables are tender-crisp.
7. Stir in the chopped fresh basil leaves.
8. Serve the Thai basil tofu stir-fry hot over cooked jasmine rice.

Nutrition Info (per serving, excluding rice):
- Calories: 180
- Carbohydrates: 12g
- Protein: 14g
- Fat: 9g
- Fiber: 4g
- Sugar: 6g

Recipe 17: Air Fried Lemon Garlic Shrimp and Asparagus
Cooking Time: 12 minutes
Servings: 4
Ingredients:
- 1 lb large shrimp, peeled and deveined
- 1 bunch asparagus spears, trimmed
- 2 tablespoons olive oil
- Zest and juice of 1 lemon
- 3 cloves garlic, minced
- 1/2 teaspoon dried thyme
- Salt and pepper to taste

Instructions:
1. Preheat your air fryer to 375°F (190°C) for 2 minutes.
2. In a bowl, combine the olive oil, lemon zest, lemon juice, minced garlic, dried thyme, salt, and pepper.
3. Toss the shrimp and trimmed asparagus spears in the lemon garlic mixture until they are well coated.
4. Place the shrimp and asparagus in the air fryer basket in a single layer.
5. Air fry at 375°F (190°C) for 8-10 minutes, shaking the basket halfway through, or until the shrimp are pink and cooked through, and the asparagus is tender.
6. Serve the lemon garlic shrimp and asparagus hot.

Nutrition Info (per serving):
- Calories: 180
- Carbohydrates: 6g
- Protein: 24g
- Fat: 7g
- Fiber: 3g
- Sugar: 2g

RECIPE 18: AIR FRIED BUTTERMILK FRIED CHICKEN

Cooking Time: 25 minutes
Servings: 4
Ingredients:
- 4 bone-in, skin-on chicken thighs
- 1 cup buttermilk
- 1 cup breadcrumbs (whole wheat for a healthier option)
- 1 teaspoon paprika
- 1/2 teaspoon garlic powder
- 1/2 teaspoon onion powder
- Salt and pepper to taste
- Cooking spray for the air fryer basket

Instructions:
1. Preheat your air fryer to 375°F (190°C) for 2 minutes.
2. In a bowl, combine the buttermilk, paprika, garlic powder, onion powder, salt, and pepper.
3. Dip each chicken thigh into the buttermilk mixture, allowing any excess to drip off.
4. In a separate bowl, mix the breadcrumbs with a bit of additional paprika, garlic powder, onion powder, salt, and pepper.
5. Dredge each chicken thigh in the breadcrumb mixture, pressing the breadcrumbs onto the chicken to adhere.
6. Lightly grease the air fryer basket with cooking spray.
7. Place the breaded chicken thighs in the air fryer basket, skin-side down.
8. Air fry at 375°F (190°C) for 20-25 minutes, turning the chicken halfway through, or until the chicken is cooked through, crispy, and golden.
9. Serve the buttermilk fried chicken hot.

Nutrition Info (per serving):
- Calories: 350
- Carbohydrates: 20g
- Protein: 24g
- Fat: 19g
- Fiber: 1g
- Sugar: 3g

RECIPE 19: AIR FRIED QUINOA AND BLACK BEAN STUFFED PEPPERS

Cooking Time: 20 minutes
Servings: 4
Ingredients:

- 4 large bell peppers, any color
- 1 cup cooked quinoa
- 1 cup canned black beans, drained and rinsed
- 1 cup corn kernels (fresh, frozen, or canned)
- 1/2 cup diced tomatoes
- 1/2 cup diced red onion
- 1/2 cup shredded low-fat cheddar cheese
- 1 teaspoon chili powder
- Salt and pepper to taste
- Cooking spray for the air fryer basket

Instructions:

1. Preheat your air fryer to 350°F (180°C) for 2 minutes.
2. Cut the tops off the bell peppers and remove the seeds.
3. In a bowl, mix the cooked quinoa, black beans, corn, diced tomatoes, diced red onion, shredded cheddar cheese, chili powder, salt, and pepper.
4. Stuff each bell pepper with the quinoa and black bean mixture.
5. Lightly grease the air fryer basket with cooking spray.
6. Place the stuffed bell peppers in the air fryer basket.
7. Air fry at 350°F (180°C) for 18-20 minutes, or until the peppers are tender and the filling is heated through.
8. Serve the quinoa and black bean stuffed peppers hot as a nutritious main course.

Nutrition Info (per serving):

- Calories: 290
- Carbohydrates: 49g
- Protein: 13g
- Fat: 4g
- Fiber: 11g
- Sugar: 7g

RECIPE 20: AIR FRIED TERIYAKI CHICKEN AND VEGETABLE SKEWERS

Cooking Time: 15 minutes
Servings: 4
Ingredients:

- 1 lb boneless, skinless chicken breasts, cubed
- 2 cups mixed vegetables (such as bell peppers, zucchini, cherry tomatoes), cut into chunks
- 1/4 cup low-sodium soy sauce
- 2 tablespoons honey (or a sugar-free sweetener)
- 1 tablespoon rice vinegar
- 2 cloves garlic, minced
- 1 teaspoon grated ginger
- Wooden skewers, soaked in water
- Cooked brown rice for serving

Instructions:
1. Preheat your air fryer to 375°F (190°C) for 2 minutes.
2. In a bowl, whisk together the soy sauce, honey, rice vinegar, minced garlic, and grated ginger.
3. Thread the chicken cubes and mixed vegetables onto the wooden skewers, alternating between chicken and vegetables.
4. Brush the skewers with the teriyaki sauce until they are well coated.
5. Place the skewers in the air fryer basket.
6. Air fry at 375°F (190°C) for 12-15 minutes, turning the skewers occasionally, or until the chicken is cooked through and the vegetables are tender.
7. Serve the teriyaki chicken and vegetable skewers hot over cooked brown rice.

Nutrition Info (per serving, excluding rice):
- Calories: 220
- Carbohydrates: 16g
- Protein: 26g
- Fat: 3g
- Fiber: 2g
- Sugar: 12g

Chapter 7: Sides and Vegetables

Recipe 1: Roasted Brussels Sprouts with Balsamic Reduction
Cooking Time: 15 minutes
Servings: 4
Ingredients:
- 1 lb Brussels sprouts, trimmed and halved
- 2 tablespoons olive oil
- Salt and pepper to taste
- 2 tablespoons balsamic vinegar
- 1 tablespoon honey (or a sugar-free sweetener)
- 1 clove garlic, minced

Instructions:
1. Preheat your air fryer to 375°F (190°C) for 2 minutes.
2. In a bowl, toss the halved Brussels sprouts with olive oil, salt, and pepper until they are well coated.
3. Place the Brussels sprouts in the air fryer basket in a single layer.
4. Air fry at 375°F (190°C) for 12-15 minutes, shaking the basket halfway through, or until the Brussels sprouts are crispy and browned.
5. In the last 2 minutes of air frying, combine balsamic vinegar, honey, and minced garlic in a small saucepan. Heat over low heat until it thickens into a reduction.
6. Drizzle the balsamic reduction over the air-fried Brussels sprouts.
7. Serve the roasted Brussels sprouts hot as a delightful side dish.

Nutrition Info (per serving):
- Calories: 100
- Carbohydrates: 12g
- Protein: 3g
- Fat: 5g
- Fiber: 4g
- Sugar: 5g

Recipe 2: Garlic Parmesan Air Fried Asparagus
Cooking Time: 10 minutes
Servings: 4
Ingredients:
- 1 lb asparagus spears, trimmed
- 2 tablespoons olive oil
- 2 cloves garlic, minced
- 1/4 cup grated Parmesan cheese
- Salt and pepper to taste
- Lemon wedges for serving (optional)

Instructions:
1. Preheat your air fryer to 375°F (190°C) for 2 minutes.
2. In a bowl, toss the trimmed asparagus with olive oil, minced garlic, grated Parmesan cheese, salt, and pepper until they are well coated.

3. Place the seasoned asparagus in the air fryer basket in a single layer.
4. Air fry at 375°F (190°C) for 8-10 minutes, shaking the basket halfway through, or until the asparagus is tender and the cheese is golden and crispy.
5. Squeeze lemon wedges over the air-fried asparagus before serving if desired.
6. Serve the garlic Parmesan air fried asparagus hot as a flavorful side dish.

Nutrition Info (per serving):
- Calories: 90
- Carbohydrates: 5g
- Protein: 4g
- Fat: 7g
- Fiber: 2g
- Sugar: 2g

RECIPE 3: SPICY ROASTED CAULIFLOWER BITES
Cooking Time: 15 minutes
Servings: 4
Ingredients:
- 1 head cauliflower, cut into bite-sized florets
- 2 tablespoons olive oil
- 1 teaspoon chili powder (adjust to taste)
- 1/2 teaspoon paprika
- 1/2 teaspoon cumin
- 1/4 teaspoon garlic powder
- Salt and pepper to taste
- Cooking spray for the air fryer basket

Instructions:
1. Preheat your air fryer to 375°F (190°C) for 2 minutes.
2. In a bowl, toss the cauliflower florets with olive oil, chili powder, paprika, cumin, garlic powder, salt, and pepper until they are well coated.
3. Lightly grease the air fryer basket with cooking spray.
4. Place the seasoned cauliflower florets in the air fryer basket in a single layer.
5. Air fry at 375°F (190°C) for 12-15 minutes, shaking the basket halfway through, or until the cauliflower is tender and crispy.
6. Serve the spicy roasted cauliflower bites hot as a zesty side dish.

Nutrition Info (per serving):
- Calories: 70
- Carbohydrates: 7g
- Protein: 3g
- Fat: 4g
- Fiber: 3g
- Sugar: 2g

RECIPE 4: AIR FRIED SWEET POTATO FRIES
Cooking Time: 15 minutes
Servings: 4
Ingredients:
- 2 large sweet potatoes cut into fries
- 2 tablespoons olive oil
- 1 teaspoon paprika
- 1/2 teaspoon garlic powder
- Salt and pepper to taste
- Cooking spray for the air fryer basket

Instructions:
1. Preheat your air fryer to 375°F (190°C) for 2 minutes.
2. In a bowl, toss the sweet potato fries with olive oil, paprika, garlic powder, salt, and pepper until they are well coated.
3. Lightly grease the air fryer basket with cooking spray.
4. Place the seasoned sweet potato fries in the air fryer basket in a single layer.
5. Air fry at 375°F (190°C) for 12-15 minutes, shaking the basket halfway through, or until the sweet potato fries are crispy and browned.
6. Serve the air fried sweet potato fries hot as a delicious side.

Nutrition Info (per serving):
- Calories: 150
- Carbohydrates: 25g
- Protein: 2g
- Fat: 5g
- Fiber: 4g
- Sugar: 6g

RECIPE 5: AIR FRIED GARLIC PARMESAN BRUSSELS SPROUTS
Cooking Time: 15 minutes
Servings: 4
Ingredients:
- 1 lb Brussels sprouts, trimmed and halved
- 2 tablespoons olive oil
- 2 cloves garlic, minced
- 1/4 cup grated Parmesan cheese
- Salt and pepper to taste
- Lemon wedges for serving (optional)

Instructions:
1. Preheat your air fryer to 375°F (190°C) for 2 minutes.
2. In a bowl, toss the halved Brussels sprouts with olive oil, minced garlic, grated Parmesan cheese, salt, and pepper until they are well coated.
3. Place the seasoned Brussels sprouts in the air fryer basket in a single layer.
4. Air fry at 375°F (190°C) for 12-15 minutes, shaking the basket halfway through, or until the Brussels sprouts are crispy and the cheese is golden.
5. Squeeze lemon wedges over the air-fried Brussels sprouts before serving if desired.
6. Serve the garlic Parmesan air fried Brussels sprouts hot as a flavorful side dish.

Nutrition Info (per serving):

- Calories: 120
- Carbohydrates: 10g
- Protein: 5g
- Fat: 7g
- Fiber: 4g
- Sugar: 2g

RECIPE 6: AIR FRIED ZUCCHINI CHIPS
Cooking Time: 12 minutes
Servings: 4
Ingredients:
- 2 large zucchinis, thinly sliced into rounds
- 2 tablespoons olive oil
- 1/4 cup grated Parmesan cheese
- 1/2 teaspoon garlic powder
- 1/2 teaspoon dried oregano
- Salt and pepper to taste
- Cooking spray for the air fryer basket

Instructions:
1. Preheat your air fryer to 375°F (190°C) for 2 minutes.
2. In a bowl, toss the zucchini slices with olive oil, grated Parmesan cheese, garlic powder, dried oregano, salt, and pepper until they are well coated.
3. Lightly grease the air fryer basket with cooking spray.
4. Place the seasoned zucchini slices in the air fryer basket in a single layer.
5. Air fry at 375°F (190°C) for 10-12 minutes, flipping the zucchini slices halfway through, or until they are crispy and golden.
6. Serve the air fried zucchini chips hot as a tasty side or snack.

Nutrition Info (per serving):
- Calories: 90
- Carbohydrates: 5g
- Protein: 3g
- Fat: 7g
- Fiber: 2g
- Sugar: 2g

RECIPE 7: AIR FRIED GARLIC HERB MUSHROOMS
Cooking Time: 12 minutes
Servings: 4
Ingredients:
- 1 lb button mushrooms, cleaned and halved
- 2 tablespoons olive oil
- 2 cloves garlic, minced
- 1 teaspoon dried thyme
- 1 teaspoon dried rosemary
- Salt and pepper to taste
- Fresh parsley for garnish (optional)

Instructions:

1. Preheat your air fryer to 375°F (190°C) for 2 minutes.
2. In a bowl, toss the halved mushrooms with olive oil, minced garlic, dried thyme, dried rosemary, salt, and pepper until they are well coated.
3. Place the seasoned mushrooms in the air fryer basket in a single layer.
4. Air fry at 375°F (190°C) for 10-12 minutes, shaking the basket halfway through, or until the mushrooms are tender and browned.
5. Garnish with fresh parsley before serving if desired.
6. Serve the garlic herb air fried mushrooms hot as a delightful side.

Nutrition Info (per serving):
- Calories: 80
- Carbohydrates: 4g
- Protein: 3g
- Fat: 7g
- Fiber: 1g
- Sugar: 2g

RECIPE 8: AIR FRIED BUTTERY CORN ON THE COB
Cooking Time: 10 minutes
Servings: 4
Ingredients:
- 4 ears of corn, husked and halved
- 2 tablespoons unsalted butter, melted
- Salt and pepper to taste

Instructions:
1. Preheat your air fryer to 375°F (190°C) for 2 minutes.
2. Brush each ear of corn with melted butter and season with salt and pepper.
3. Place the corn halves in the air fryer basket.
4. Air fry at 375°F (190°C) for 8-10 minutes, turning the corn halfway through, or until the corn is tender and lightly charred.
5. Serve the buttery air fried corn on the cob hot.

Nutrition Info (per serving):
- Calories: 120
- Carbohydrates: 15g
- Protein: 2g
- Fat: 7g
- Fiber: 2g
- Sugar: 4g

Recipe 9: Air Fried Herb-Roasted Potatoes

Cooking Time: 20 minutes
Servings: 4
Ingredients:
- 1 lb baby potatoes, halved
- 2 tablespoons olive oil
- 1 teaspoon dried rosemary
- 1 teaspoon dried thyme
- 1 teaspoon garlic powder
- Salt and pepper to taste

Instructions:
- Preheat your air fryer to 375°F (190°C) for 2 minutes.
- In a bowl, toss the halved baby potatoes with olive oil, dried rosemary, dried thyme, garlic powder, salt, and pepper until they are well coated.
- Place the seasoned potatoes in the air fryer basket in a single layer.
- Air fry at 375°F (190°C) for 18-20 minutes, shaking the basket halfway through, or until the potatoes are crispy and golden.
- Serve the herb-roasted air fried potatoes hot as a savory side.

Nutrition Info (per serving):
- Calories: 120
- Carbohydrates: 15g
- Protein: 2g
- Fat: 7g
- Fiber: 2g
- Sugar: 1g

Recipe 10: Air Fried Green Beans with Almonds

Cooking Time: 12 minutes
Servings: 4
Ingredients:
- 1 lb fresh green beans, trimmed
- 2 tablespoons olive oil
- 1/4 cup sliced almonds
- 1 teaspoon lemon zest
- Salt and pepper to taste

Instructions:
- Preheat your air fryer to 375°F (190°C) for 2 minutes.
- In a bowl, toss the trimmed green beans with olive oil, sliced almonds, lemon zest, salt, and pepper until they are well coated.
- Place the seasoned green beans in the air fryer basket in a single layer.
- Air fry at 375°F (190°C) for 10-12 minutes, shaking the basket halfway through, or until the green beans are tender-crisp and the almonds are toasted.
- Serve the air fried green beans with almonds hot.

Nutrition Info (per serving):
- Calories: 90
- Carbohydrates: 6g

- Protein: 2g
- Fat: 7g
- Fiber: 3g
- Sugar: 2g

RECIPE 11: AIR FRIED RATATOUILLE
Cooking Time: 15 minutes
Servings: 4
Ingredients:
- 1 medium eggplant, diced
- 2 medium zucchinis, diced
- 2 bell peppers (red and yellow), diced
- 1 red onion, diced
- 2 cloves garlic, minced
- 2 tablespoons olive oil
- 1 teaspoon dried basil
- 1 teaspoon dried thyme
- Salt and pepper to taste

Instructions:
1. Preheat your air fryer to 375°F (190°C) for 2 minutes.
2. In a bowl, combine the diced eggplant, zucchinis, bell peppers, red onion, minced garlic, olive oil, dried basil, dried thyme, salt, and pepper.
3. Place the mixture in the air fryer basket.
4. Air fry at 375°F (190°C) for 12-15 minutes, shaking the basket halfway through, or until the vegetables are tender and lightly browned.
5. Serve the air fried ratatouille as a delicious side dish.

Nutrition Info (per serving):
- Calories: 120
- Carbohydrates: 15g
- Protein: 3g
- Fat: 7g
- Fiber: 5g
- Sugar: 8g

RECIPE 12: AIR FRIED HONEY GLAZED CARROTS
Cooking Time: 12 minutes
Servings: 4
Ingredients:
- 1 lb baby carrots
- 2 tablespoons honey
- 1 tablespoon olive oil
- 1/2 teaspoon ground cinnamon
- Salt and pepper to taste

Instructions:
1. Preheat your air fryer to 375°F (190°C) for 2 minutes.
2. In a bowl, toss the baby carrots with honey, olive oil, ground cinnamon, salt, and pepper until they are well coated.

3. Place the seasoned carrots in the air fryer basket in a single layer.
4. Air fry at 375°F (190°C) for 10-12 minutes, shaking the basket halfway through, or until the carrots are tender and glazed.
5. Serve the honey glazed air fried carrots hot.

Nutrition Info (per serving):
- Calories: 80
- Carbohydrates: 15g
- Protein: 1g
- Fat: 3g
- Fiber: 3g
- Sugar: 11g

RECIPE 13: AIR FRIED LEMON GARLIC BROCCOLI

Cooking Time: 10 minutes
Servings: 4
Ingredients:
- 1 lb broccoli florets
- 2 tablespoons olive oil
- Zest and juice of 1 lemon
- 2 cloves garlic, minced
- Salt and pepper to taste

Instructions:
1. Preheat your air fryer to 375°F (190°C) for 2 minutes.
2. In a bowl, toss the broccoli florets with olive oil, lemon zest, lemon juice, minced garlic, salt, and pepper until they are well coated.
3. Place the seasoned broccoli florets in the air fryer basket in a single layer.
4. Air fry at 375°F (190°C) for 8-10 minutes, shaking the basket halfway through, or until the broccoli is tender and lightly browned.
5. Serve the lemon garlic air fried broccoli hot.

Nutrition Info (per serving):
- Calories: 80
- Carbohydrates: 7g
- Protein: 3g
- Fat: 6g
- Fiber: 3g
- Sugar: 2g

RECIPE 14: AIR FRIED CILANTRO LIME CORN

Cooking Time: 12 minutes
Servings: 4
Ingredients:
- 4 ears of corn, husked and halved
- 2 tablespoons olive oil
- Zest and juice of 1 lime
- 1/4 cup fresh cilantro leaves, chopped
- Salt and pepper to taste

Instructions:

1. Preheat your air fryer to 375°F (190°C) for 2 minutes.
2. Brush each ear of corn with olive oil and season with salt and pepper.
3. Place the corn halves in the air fryer basket.
4. Air fry at 375°F (190°C) for 10-12 minutes, turning the corn halfway through, or until the corn is tender and lightly charred.
5. Sprinkle the fresh cilantro leaves over the air-fried corn and drizzle with lime zest and juice.
6. Serve the cilantro lime air fried corn hot as a flavorful side.

Nutrition Info (per serving):

- Calories: 120
- Carbohydrates: 20g
- Protein: 3g
- Fat: 5g
- Fiber: 3g
- Sugar: 6g

RECIPE 15: AIR FRIED SESAME GINGER GREEN BEANS
Cooking Time: 12 minutes
Servings: 4
Ingredients:

- 1 lb fresh green beans, trimmed
- 2 tablespoons olive oil
- 2 tablespoons low-sodium soy sauce
- 1 tablespoon sesame oil
- 1 tablespoon rice vinegar
- 1 tablespoon honey (or a sugar-free sweetener)
- 1 teaspoon grated ginger
- 1 teaspoon sesame seeds
- Salt and pepper to taste

Instructions:
1. Preheat your air fryer to 375°F (190°C) for 2 minutes.
2. In a bowl, toss the trimmed green beans with olive oil, low-sodium soy sauce, sesame oil, rice vinegar, honey, grated ginger, sesame seeds, salt, and pepper until they are well coated.
3. Place the seasoned green beans in the air fryer basket in a single layer.
4. Air fry at 375°F (190°C) for 10-12 minutes, shaking the basket halfway through, or until the green beans are tender-crisp and glazed.
5. Serve the sesame ginger air fried green beans hot.

Nutrition Info (per serving):

- Calories: 90
- Carbohydrates: 10g
- Protein: 2g
- Fat: 6g
- Fiber: 3g
- Sugar: 6g

Chapter 8: Desserts and Treats

Recipe 1: Cinnamon Apple Chips
Cooking Time: 10 minutes
Servings: 4
Ingredients:
- 2 apples, thinly sliced
- 1 teaspoon ground cinnamon
- 1 tablespoon granulated sugar (or a sugar-free sweetener)

Instructions:
1. Preheat your air fryer to 350°F (175°C) for 2 minutes.
2. In a bowl, toss the thinly sliced apples with ground cinnamon and granulated sugar until they are well coated.
3. Place the coated apple slices in the air fryer basket in a single layer.
4. Air fry at 350°F (175°C) for 8-10 minutes, flipping the apple slices halfway through, or until they are crispy and lightly browned.
5. Allow the cinnamon apple chips to cool before serving.

Nutrition Info (per serving):
- Calories: 70
- Carbohydrates: 18g
- Protein: 0g
- Fat: 0g
- Fiber: 3g
- Sugar: 14g

Recipe 2: Chocolate Avocado Pudding
Preparation Time: 10 minutes
Chilling Time: 2 hours
Servings: 4
Ingredients:
- 2 ripe avocados, peeled and pitted
- 1/4 cup unsweetened cocoa powder
- 1/4 cup maple syrup (or a sugar-free sweetener)
- 1/4 cup almond milk (or any milk of choice)
- 1 teaspoon vanilla extract
- Pinch of salt
- Fresh berries for garnish (optional)

Instructions:
1. In a blender or food processor, combine the ripe avocados, unsweetened cocoa powder, maple syrup, almond milk, vanilla extract, and a pinch of salt.
2. Blend until the mixture is smooth and creamy.
3. Transfer the chocolate avocado pudding to individual serving bowls or glasses.
4. Refrigerate for at least 2 hours to chill and set.
5. Garnish with fresh berries before serving if desired.

Nutrition Info (per serving):
- Calories: 200
- Carbohydrates: 22g
- Protein: 3g
- Fat: 13g
- Fiber: 7g
- Sugar: 11g

RECIPE 3: MIXED BERRY CRISP

Cooking Time: 20 minutes
Servings: 4
Ingredients:
- 2 cups mixed berries (such as strawberries, blueberries, and raspberries)
- 1/4 cup rolled oats
- 2 tablespoons almond flour (or any flour of choice)
- 2 tablespoons granulated sugar (or a sugar-free sweetener)
- 1/2 teaspoon ground cinnamon
- 2 tablespoons unsalted butter, cubed (or coconut oil for a dairy-free option)
- Vanilla ice cream or whipped cream for serving (optional)

Instructions:
1. Preheat your air fryer to 350°F (175°C) for 2 minutes.
2. In a bowl, combine the mixed berries with 1 tablespoon of granulated sugar. Toss to coat the berries.
3. In another bowl, mix the rolled oats, almond flour, remaining 1 tablespoon of granulated sugar, and ground cinnamon.
4. Add the cubed unsalted butter (or coconut oil) to the oat mixture and use your fingers to work it in until the mixture resembles coarse crumbs.
5. Divide the sugared mixed berries among four ramekins or oven-safe dishes.
6. Sprinkle the oat mixture evenly over the berries.
7. Place the ramekins in the air fryer basket. You may need to cook them in batches if they don't all fit at once.
8. Air fry at 350°F (175°C) for 15-20 minutes or until the topping is golden brown and the berries are bubbling.
9. Allow the mixed berry crisp to cool for a few minutes before serving.
10. Serve with a scoop of vanilla ice cream or a dollop of whipped cream if desired.

Nutrition Info (per serving, without ice cream or whipped cream):
- Calories: 160
- Carbohydrates: 24g
- Protein: 2g
- Fat: 7g
- Fiber: 4g
- Sugar: 13g

RECIPE 4: AIR FRIED BANANA FRITTERS

Cooking Time: 10 minutes
Servings: 4
Ingredients:

- 4 ripe bananas, peeled and sliced into rounds
- 1/2 cup all-purpose flour (or almond flour for a gluten-free option)
- 1/4 cup unsweetened shredded coconut
- 2 tablespoons granulated sugar (or a sugar-free sweetener)
- 1 teaspoon ground cinnamon
- 1/4 cup milk (or a dairy-free milk of choice)
- Cooking spray for the air fryer basket

Instructions:

1. Preheat your air fryer to 350°F (175°C) for 2 minutes.
2. In a bowl, combine the flour, shredded coconut, granulated sugar, and ground cinnamon.
3. Gradually add the milk to the dry ingredients, whisking until you have a smooth batter.
4. Dip the banana slices into the batter, ensuring they are well coated.
5. Lightly grease the air fryer basket with cooking spray.
6. Place the coated banana slices in the air fryer basket in a single layer.
7. Air fry at 350°F (175°C) for 8-10 minutes, flipping the fritters halfway through, or until they are crispy and golden.
8. Serve the air fried banana fritters warm.

Nutrition Info (per serving):

- Calories: 150
- Carbohydrates: 33g
- Protein: 2g
- Fat: 2g
- Fiber: 3g
- Sugar: 15g

RECIPE 5: AIR FRIED MINI CHURROS

Cooking Time: 12 minutes
Servings: 4
Ingredients:

- 1/2 cup water
- 2 tablespoons unsalted butter
- 2 tablespoons granulated sugar (or a sugar-free sweetener)
- 1/2 cup all-purpose flour (or almond flour for a gluten-free option)
- 1/2 teaspoon ground cinnamon
- 1/4 teaspoon salt
- Cooking spray for the air fryer basket

For Cinnamon Sugar Coating:

- 1/4 cup granulated sugar (or a sugar-free sweetener)
- 1 teaspoon ground cinnamon

Instructions:

1. In a saucepan, combine the water, unsalted butter, and granulated sugar. Bring to a boil over medium heat.
2. Remove the saucepan from the heat and add the flour, ground cinnamon, and salt. Stir vigorously until the mixture forms a smooth dough.
3. Allow the dough to cool for a few minutes.
4. Preheat your air fryer to 350°F (175°C) for 2 minutes.
5. Scoop the dough into a piping bag fitted with a star tip.
6. Pipe the dough into 4-inch churros onto a parchment paper-lined tray.
7. Lightly grease the air fryer basket with cooking spray.
8. Place the churros in the air fryer basket in a single layer.
9. Air fry at 350°F (175°C) for 10-12 minutes, turning the churros halfway through, or until they are crispy and lightly browned.
10. In a bowl, mix together the granulated sugar and ground cinnamon for the coating.
11. While the churros are still warm, roll them in the cinnamon sugar mixture to coat.
12. Serve the air fried mini churros hot with chocolate dipping sauce if desired.

Nutrition Info (per serving):
- Calories: 160
- Carbohydrates: 25g
- Protein: 2g
- Fat: 6g
- Fiber: 1g
- Sugar: 11g

RECIPE 6: AIR FRIED STRAWBERRY SHORTCAKE

Cooking Time: 10 minutes
Servings: 4
Ingredients:
- 4 slices of angel food cake
- 1 cup fresh strawberries, sliced
- 1 cup whipped cream
- 1 tablespoon powdered sugar (optional for garnish)
- Mint leaves for garnish (optional)

Instructions:
1. Preheat your air fryer to 350°F (175°C) for 2 minutes.
2. Place the slices of angel food cake in the air fryer basket.
3. Air fry at 350°F (175°C) for 4-5 minutes, or until the cake is toasted and slightly crispy.
4. Remove the toasted angel food cake from the air fryer.
5. To assemble, place a slice of toasted angel food cake on each serving plate.
6. Top with sliced strawberries.
7. Add a dollop of whipped cream on top of the strawberries.
8. Dust with powdered sugar and garnish with mint leaves if desired.
9. Serve the air fried strawberry shortcake immediately.

NUTRITION INFO (PER SERVING, WITHOUT POWDERED SUGAR):
- Calories: 220
- Carbohydrates: 46g
- Protein: 3g
- Fat: 3g

- Fiber: 2g
- Sugar: 18g

Recipe 7: Air Fried Peach Cobbler

Cooking Time: 20 minutes
Servings: 4
Ingredients:
- 2 cups canned or fresh peaches, sliced
- 1/2 cup all-purpose flour
- 1/2 cup granulated sugar (or a sugar-free sweetener)
- 1/2 teaspoon baking powder
- 1/4 teaspoon salt
- 1/2 cup milk (or a dairy-free milk of choice)
- 1/4 cup unsalted butter, melted (or coconut oil for a dairy-free option)
- 1/2 teaspoon ground cinnamon
- Vanilla ice cream for serving (optional)

Instructions:
1. Preheat your air fryer to 350°F (175°C) for 2 minutes.
2. In a bowl, combine the sliced peaches with 1/4 cup of granulated sugar. Toss to coat the peaches.
3. In another bowl, mix the flour, remaining 1/4 cup of granulated sugar, baking powder, and salt.
4. Add the milk and melted unsalted butter (or coconut oil) to the dry ingredients. Stir until you have a smooth batter.
5. Grease a 6-inch round oven-safe dish that fits in your air fryer.
6. Pour the peach slices into the greased dish.
7. Pour the batter evenly over the peaches.
8. Sprinkle ground cinnamon over the top.
9. Place the dish in the air fryer basket.
10. Air fry at 350°F (175°C) for 18-20 minutes or until the cobbler is golden brown and bubbly.
11. Allow the air fried peach cobbler to cool slightly before serving.
12. Serve warm with a scoop of vanilla ice cream if desired.

Nutrition Info (per serving, without ice cream):
- Calories: 350
- Carbohydrates: 65g
- Protein: 4g
- Fat: 10g
- Fiber: 3g
- Sugar: 43g

Recipe 8: Air Fried Peanut Butter Banana Bites

Cooking Time: 8 minutes
Servings: 4
Ingredients:
- 2 bananas, peeled and cut into 1-inch slices
- 2 tablespoons peanut butter (or almond butter for a nut-free option)
- 1/4 cup granola
- Cooking spray for the air fryer basket

Instructions:

1. Preheat your air fryer to 350°F (175°C) for 2 minutes.
2. Spread a small amount of peanut butter on one side of each banana slice.
3. Press granola onto the peanut butter-covered side of each banana slice to create a topping.
4. Lightly grease the air fryer basket with cooking spray.
5. Place the banana bites in the air fryer basket.
6. Air fry at 350°F (175°C) for 6-8 minutes, or until the banana bites are warm and slightly crispy.
7. Serve the air fried peanut butter banana bites as a delicious treat.

Nutrition Info (per serving):
- Calories: 120
- Carbohydrates: 21g
- Protein: 3g
- Fat: 4g
- Fiber: 2g
- Sugar: 10g

RECIPE 9: AIR FRIED S'MORES
Cooking Time: 3 minutes
Servings: 4
Ingredients:
- 4 graham cracker squares
- 4 marshmallows
- 4 squares of chocolate (about 1 ounce each)
- Cooking spray for the air fryer basket

Instructions:
1. Preheat your air fryer to 350°F (175°C) for 2 minutes.
2. Place a marshmallow on top of each graham cracker square.
3. Add a square of chocolate on top of each marshmallow.
4. Top each stack with another graham cracker square to create a sandwich.
5. Lightly grease the air fryer basket with cooking spray.
6. Place the s'mores in the air fryer basket.
7. Air fry at 350°F (175°C) for 2-3 minutes, or until the marshmallows are gooey and slightly toasted.
8. Serve the air fried s'mores as a classic campfire treat.

RECIPE 10: AIR FRIED BLUEBERRY HAND PIES
Cooking Time: 15 minutes
Servings: 4
Ingredients:
- 1 sheet of refrigerated pie crust dough
- 1/2 cup blueberry pie filling (store-bought or homemade)
- 1 egg, beaten
- Powdered sugar for dusting (optional)

Instructions:
1. Preheat your air fryer to 375°F (190°C) for 2 minutes.
2. Unroll the refrigerated pie crust dough and cut it into 4 equal squares.
3. Place a spoonful of blueberry pie filling in the center of each square.
4. Fold the dough over the filling to create a triangle and press the edges to seal.
5. Brush each hand pie with beaten egg.
6. Lightly grease the air fryer basket with cooking spray.

7. Place the hand pies in the air fryer basket.
8. Air fry at 375°F (190°C) for 12-15 minutes, or until the hand pies are golden brown and the filling is bubbling.
9. Allow the air fried blueberry hand pies to cool slightly before serving.
10. Dust with powdered sugar if desired.

Nutrition Info (per serving, without powdered sugar):
- Calories: 280
- Carbohydrates: 41g
- Protein: 3g
- Fat: 12g
- Fiber: 1g
- Sugar: 15g

RECIPE 11: AIR FRIED MINI APPLE PIES
Cooking Time: 15 minutes
Servings: 4
Ingredients:
- 1 sheet of refrigerated pie crust dough
- 1 cup apple pie filling (store-bought or homemade)
- 1 egg, beaten
- Caramel sauce for drizzling (optional)

Instructions:
1. Preheat your air fryer to 375°F (190°C) for 2 minutes.
2. Unroll the refrigerated pie crust dough and cut it into 4 equal squares.
3. Place a spoonful of apple pie filling in the center of each square.
4. Fold the dough over the filling to create a triangle and press the edges to seal.
5. Brush each mini apple pie with beaten egg.
6. Lightly grease the air fryer basket with cooking spray.
7. Place the mini apple pies in the air fryer basket.
8. Air fry at 375°F (190°C) for 12-15 minutes, or until the pies are golden brown and the filling is bubbling.
9. Allow the air fried mini apple pies to cool slightly before serving.
10. Drizzle with caramel sauce if desired.

RECIPE 12: AIR FRIED CHOCOLATE CHIP COOKIES
Cooking Time: 8 minutes
Servings: 4
Ingredients:
- 1/2 cup unsalted butter, softened
- 1/2 cup granulated sugar
- 1/4 cup brown sugar
- 1 egg
- 1 teaspoon vanilla extract
- 1 1/4 cups all-purpose flour
- 1/2 teaspoon baking soda
- 1/4 teaspoon salt
- 1/2 cup chocolate chips

Instructions:
1. In a mixing bowl, cream together the softened unsalted butter, granulated sugar, and brown sugar until light and fluffy.
2. Beat in the egg and vanilla extract until well combined.
3. In a separate bowl, whisk together the all-purpose flour, baking soda, and salt.
4. Gradually add the dry ingredients to the wet ingredients and mix until a cookie dough forms.
5. Stir in the chocolate chips.
6. Preheat your air fryer to 350°F (175°C) for 2 minutes.
7. Drop rounded tablespoons of cookie dough onto the air fryer tray, leaving space between each cookie.
8. Air fry at 350°F (175°C) for 6-8 minutes, or until the cookies are golden around the edges.
9. Allow the air fried chocolate chip cookies to cool on a wire rack before serving.

Nutrition Info (per serving, 1 cookie):
- Calories: 280
- Carbohydrates: 37g
- Protein: 2g
- Fat: 14g
- Fiber: 1g
- Sugar: 22g

RECIPE 13: AIR FRIED LEMON BARS
Cooking Time: 20 minutes
Servings: 4
Ingredients:
- 1 cup all-purpose flour
- 1/2 cup unsalted butter, softened
- 1/4 cup powdered sugar
- 2 large eggs
- 1 cup granulated sugar
- 2 tablespoons all-purpose flour
- 2 tablespoons lemon juice
- Zest of 1 lemon
- Powdered sugar for dusting

Instructions:
- In a mixing bowl, combine 1 cup of all-purpose flour, softened unsalted butter, and 1/4 cup of powdered sugar. Mix until crumbly.
- Press the mixture into the bottom of an 8x8-inch greased baking dish.
- Bake the crust in the preheated air fryer at 350°F (175°C) for 8 minutes.
- In another bowl, beat together the eggs, granulated sugar, 2 tablespoons of all-purpose flour, lemon juice, and lemon zest until well combined.
- Pour the lemon mixture over the baked crust.
- Return the dish to the air fryer.
- Air fry at 350°F (175°C) for an additional 12 minutes or until the lemon bars are set and lightly browned around the edges.
- Allow the air fried lemon bars to cool in the baking dish.
- Dust with powdered sugar before serving.

Recipe 14: Air Fried Chocolate-Dipped Strawberries
Cooking Time: 5 minutes
Servings: 4
Ingredients:
- 1 cup strawberries, washed and dried
- 1/2 cup dark chocolate chips
- 1 teaspoon coconut oil

Instructions:
1. Preheat your air fryer to 350°F (175°C) for 2 minutes.
2. In a microwave-safe bowl, melt the dark chocolate chips and coconut oil together in 20-second intervals, stirring until smooth.
3. Dip each strawberry into the melted chocolate, letting any excess drip off.
4. Place the chocolate-dipped strawberries in the air fryer basket.
5. Air fry at 350°F (175°C) for 3-5 minutes, or until the chocolate is set.
6. Allow the air fried chocolate-dipped strawberries to cool before serving.

Recipe 15: Air Fried Oreo Cookies
Cooking Time: 5 minutes
Servings: 4
Ingredients:
- 8 Oreo cookies
- 1/2 cup pancake mix
- 1/4 cup milk
- Cooking spray for the air fryer basket

Instructions:
1. Preheat your air fryer to 350°F (175°C) for 2 minutes.
2. In a bowl, mix together the pancake mix and milk until you have a smooth batter.
3. Dip each Oreo cookie into the batter, ensuring they are fully coated.
4. Lightly grease the air fryer basket with cooking spray.
5. Place the coated Oreo cookies in the air fryer basket in a single layer.
6. Air fry at 350°F (175°C) for 3-5 minutes, or until the cookies are golden and crispy.
7. Serve the air fried Oreo cookies hot with a scoop of ice cream if desired.

Recipe 16: Air Fried Pineapple Rings
Cooking Time: 8 minutes
Servings: 4
Ingredients:
- 4 pineapple rings (canned or fresh)
- 2 tablespoons honey
- 1/2 teaspoon ground cinnamon
- Cooking spray for the air fryer basket

Instructions:
1. Preheat your air fryer to 350°F (175°C) for 2 minutes.
2. In a bowl, combine the honey and ground cinnamon.
3. Dip each pineapple ring into the honey-cinnamon mixture, coating both sides.
4. Lightly grease the air fryer basket with cooking spray.
5. Place the coated pineapple rings in the air fryer basket.

6. Air fry at 350°F (175°C) for 6-8 minutes, flipping the rings halfway through, or until they are caramelized and slightly crispy.
   7. Serve the air fried pineapple rings warm.

RECIPE 17: AIR FRIED COCONUT MACAROONS
Cooking Time: 10 minutes
Servings: 4
Ingredients:
- 2 cups sweetened shredded coconut
- 2/3 cup sweetened condensed milk
- 1 teaspoon vanilla extract
- 1/4 teaspoon salt
- Cooking spray for the air fryer basket
- Melted chocolate for drizzling (optional)

Instructions:
1. In a bowl, combine the sweetened shredded coconut, sweetened condensed milk, vanilla extract, and salt. Mix until well combined.
2. Use a cookie scoop or your hands to form small macaroon mounds and place them on a parchment paper-lined tray.
3. Preheat your air fryer to 350°F (175°C) for 2 minutes.
4. Lightly grease the air fryer basket with cooking spray.
5. Place the macaroons in the air fryer basket in a single layer, leaving space between each one.
6. Air fry at 350°F (175°C) for 8-10 minutes, or until the macaroons are lightly golden on the outside and soft on the inside.
7. Allow the air fried coconut macaroons to cool.
8. Drizzle with melted chocolate if desired.

RECIPE 18: AIR FRIED CHURRO BITES
Cooking Time: 10 minutes
Servings: 4
Ingredients:
- 1 can refrigerated biscuit dough
- 1/4 cup granulated sugar
- 1 teaspoon ground cinnamon
- Cooking spray for the air fryer basket

Instructions:
1. Preheat your air fryer to 350°F (175°C) for 2 minutes.
2. Separate the biscuit dough into individual biscuits.
3. Cut each biscuit into 4 pieces.
4. In a bowl, mix together the granulated sugar and ground cinnamon.
5. Lightly grease the air fryer basket with cooking spray.
6. Place the biscuit pieces in the air fryer basket in a single layer.
7. Air fry at 350°F (175°C) for 6-8 minutes, or until the churro bites are golden brown and cooked through.
8. While the churro bites are still warm, toss them in the cinnamon sugar mixture to coat.
9. Serve the air fried churro bites with chocolate dipping sauce if desired.

Nutrition Info (per serving):
- Calories: 220

- Carbohydrates: 38g
- Protein: 3g
- Fat: 6g
- Fiber: 1g
- Sugar: 11g

RECIPE 19: AIR FRIED STRAWBERRY DONUTS
Cooking Time: 10 minutes
Servings: 4
Ingredients:
- 4 cake-style donuts
- 1 cup fresh strawberries, sliced
- 1/4 cup powdered sugar
- 1-2 tablespoons milk (or a dairy-free milk of choice)
- Sprinkles for garnish (optional)

Instructions:
1. Preheat your air fryer to 350°F (175°C) for 2 minutes.
2. Place the cake-style donuts in the air fryer basket.
3. Air fry at 350°F (175°C) for 4-5 minutes, or until the donuts are slightly crispy on the outside.
4. While the donuts are cooking, make the strawberry glaze. In a blender, puree the sliced strawberries until smooth. Strain the puree through a fine-mesh sieve to remove seeds.
5. In a bowl, whisk together the powdered sugar and 1-2 tablespoons of milk to create a smooth glaze.
6. Stir in the strawberry puree until well combined.
7. Once the donuts are done, dip them into the strawberry glaze, allowing any excess to drip off.
8. Garnish with sprinkles if desired.
9. Allow the air fried strawberry donuts to cool slightly before serving.

Nutrition Info (per serving, without sprinkles):
- Calories: 300
- Carbohydrates: 60g
- Protein: 3g
- Fat: 6g
- Fiber: 2g
- Sugar: 37g

RECIPE 20: AIR FRIED S'MORES STUFFED CRESCENT ROLLS
Cooking Time: 10 minutes
Servings: 4
Ingredients:
- 1 can refrigerated crescent roll dough
- 4 marshmallows
- 4 squares of chocolate (about 1 ounce each)
- Cooking spray for the air fryer basket
- Powdered sugar for dusting (optional)

Instructions:
1. Preheat your air fryer to 350°F (175°C) for 2 minutes.
2. Separate the crescent roll dough into individual triangles.
3. Place a marshmallow and a square of chocolate at the wide end of each triangle.

4. Roll up the dough, enclosing the marshmallow and chocolate, and pinch the edges to seal.
5. Lightly grease the air fryer basket with cooking spray.
6. Place the stuffed crescent rolls in the air fryer basket.
7. Air fry at 350°F (175°C) for 8-10 minutes, or until the rolls are golden brown and the marshmallow is gooey.
8. Allow the air fried s'mores stuffed crescent rolls to cool slightly.
9. Dust with powdered sugar if desired.

Nutrition Info (per serving, without powdered sugar):
- Calories: 220
- Carbohydrates: 29g
- Protein: 3g
- Fat: 10g
- Fiber: 1g
- Sugar: 14g

Chapter 9: Meal Planning and Portion Control

In this chapter, we will explore the essential aspects of meal planning and portion control, which are crucial for managing blood sugar levels effectively while enjoying a variety of delicious air-fried meals. Let's dive into some valuable tips, sample meal plans, and shopping lists to assist you on your journey to better diabetes management.

Introduction to Meal Planning and Portion Control

Meal planning and portion control are foundational elements of managing diabetes. They empower you to make informed food choices, control carbohydrate intake, and maintain steady blood sugar levels. Here are some key principles:

Balanced Meals: Aim for balanced meals that include a variety of nutrient-rich foods, such as lean proteins, whole grains, healthy fats, and plenty of vegetables.

Carbohydrate Counting: Learn to count carbohydrates to manage your blood sugar effectively. Focus on complex carbohydrates with a low glycemic index (GI) and limit simple sugars.

Fiber-Rich Foods: Incorporate high-fiber foods into your diet, like vegetables, legumes, and whole grains, as they help stabilize blood sugar levels.

Portion Control: Be mindful of portion sizes. Using measuring cups, a food scale, or your hand as a guide can help you control portions accurately.

Regular Meal Timing: Establish a routine for meals and snacks to maintain steady blood sugar levels throughout the day.

Hydration: Drink plenty of water to stay well-hydrated. Avoid sugary beverages and excessive caffeine.

Sample Meal Plans

Below are sample meal plans for a day, showcasing how to incorporate air-fried recipes into your diabetes-friendly diet. Adjust portion sizes and carbohydrate content to match your individual needs and dietary restrictions.

Breakfast:

- Air Fried Oatmeal Pancakes (2 servings)
- Scrambled eggs with spinach and tomatoes
- A small serving of Greek yogurt with berries

Morning Snack:

- A handful of raw almonds or walnuts

Lunch:

- Air Fried Chicken Salad with mixed greens, cherry tomatoes, cucumber, and a vinaigrette dressing
- A serving of quinoa or brown rice

Afternoon Snack:

- Celery and carrot sticks with hummus

Dinner:

- Lemon Herb Chicken Thighs or Balsamic Glazed Salmon
- Steamed broccoli or roasted Brussels sprouts
- A side salad with vinaigrette dressing

Evening Snack (if needed):

- Greek yogurt with a drizzle of honey

SAMPLE SHOPPING LIST

Creating a well-planned shopping list can simplify your grocery shopping and help you stay on track with your diabetes-friendly meal plan. Here's a sample shopping list:

Proteins:

- Skinless chicken thighs
- Salmon fillets
- Eggs

Vegetables:

- Mixed greens
- Spinach
- Tomatoes
- Cucumber
- Broccoli
- Brussels sprouts
- Celery
- Carrots

Fruits:

- Berries (strawberries, blueberries, raspberries)
- Lemons

Grains:

- Rolled oats
- Quinoa or brown rice

Dairy and Dairy Alternatives:

- Greek yogurt (plain, low-fat)
- Almond milk (unsweetened)

Pantry Staples:

- Olive oil (for air frying)
- Hummus
- Nuts (almonds, walnuts)
- Honey (for occasional use)
- Quinoa or brown rice (if not already stocked)

- Vinaigrette dressing (choose low-sugar or make your own)

Spices and Seasonings:

- Ground cinnamon
- Herbs (e.g., thyme, rosemary, basil)

Condiments and Sauces (if needed):

- Balsamic vinegar
- Low-sodium soy sauce (for marinades)
- Mustard (for dressings)

Chapter 10: Troubleshooting and Tips

Air frying can be a fantastic cooking method, but like any culinary technique, it comes with its challenges and quirks. In this chapter, we'll delve into common air frying issues and provide solutions to overcome them. We'll also share additional cooking tips and tricks to help you become an air frying expert.

Common Air Frying Issues and Solutions

Food Sticking to the Basket or Tray:

Solution: Use a non-stick cooking spray or parchment paper to prevent sticking. Avoid overcrowding the basket, as this can lead to food sticking together.

Food Not Getting Crispy Enough:

Solution: Ensure you preheat the air fryer, use a light coating of oil on the food, and avoid overloading the basket to allow for proper air circulation. Shake or flip the food halfway through cooking for even crispiness.

Uneven Cooking:

Solution: Arrange vfood in a single layer, ensuring pieces is not touching. If necessary, cook in batches for consistent results. Rotate or flip food halfway through cooking to ensure even cooking.

Food Drying Out:

Solution: Use a kitchen thermometer to monitor cooking times, and avoid overcooking. Baste or brush food with a little oil or sauce to keep it moist.

Breading Falling Off:

Solution: Dip food items in beaten egg or buttermilk before coating with breadcrumbs. Refrigerate coated items for 20-30 minutes to help the breading adhere better.

Smoke or Unpleasant Odors:

Solution: Clean the air fryer basket and tray regularly to prevent built-up residue from smoking. Use oils with high smoke points, like canola or grape seed oil, to minimize smoke.

Overcooking or Burning:

Solution: Pay close attention to recommended cooking times and temperatures in your recipes. Experiment with lower temperatures for delicate foods. Adjust cooking times as needed.

Foods Sticking to Each Other:

Solution: Spread food items evenly in the basket, ensuring there's enough space between them. Consider using parchment paper or silicone baking mats for items prone to sticking.

Additional Cooking Tips and Tricks

Preheat the Air Fryer: Preheating ensures even cooking and helps food become crispy. Preheat for 2-3 minutes at the desired temperature.

Use the Right Oil: Choose oils with high smoke points, such as canola, grapeseed, or avocado oil, for air frying. Lightly spray or brush oil on food for a crispy texture.

Shake or Flip: To promote even cooking and browning, shake the basket or flip food halfway through the cooking time.

Don't Overcrowd: Overloading the basket reduces air circulation and can lead to uneven cooking. Cook in batches if necessary.

Experiment with Seasonings: Get creative with seasonings, herbs, and spices to enhance flavors. Try different marinades and rubs for a variety of tastes.

Keep an Eye on Temperature: Use a kitchen thermometer to check the internal temperature of meat and poultry. The safe internal temperature varies by type of food.

Reheat Leftovers: Air fryers are excellent for reheating leftovers like pizza, fries, and chicken wings. They can revive crispiness better than a microwave.

Use Accessories: Consider using air fryer accessories like baking pans, grill racks, or silicone muffin cups for versatility in cooking.

Clean Regularly: To prevent smoke and maintain performance, clean the air fryer basket, tray, and interior after each use. Refer to the manufacturer's instructions for cleaning guidelines.

Practice Patience: Air frying may take a little trial and error to master. Keep experimenting and refining your techniques to achieve the best results.

By troubleshooting common issues and applying these tips and tricks, you'll be well-equipped to make the most of your air fryer and create delicious, crispy, and healthy meals with ease. Remember that practice makes perfect, so don't be discouraged by any initial challenges and keep exploring the culinary possibilities of your air fryer.

Conclusion

Encourage readers to embrace a healthier lifestyle through air frying and diabetic-friendly cooking.

Reiterate the importance of regular blood sugar monitoring and consulting with a healthcare professional.

Remember to consult with a registered dietitian or nutritionist to ensure the recipes and advice in the cookbook align with individual dietary needs and health goals. Additionally, it's important to stay updated with the latest diabetes management guidelines and research beyond my knowledge cutoff date, as new information may have emerged since then.

Printed in Great Britain
by Amazon